TRAVEL DIARY: SICILY

EDA HUNT

SERPENT CLUB PRESS
SCP

TRAVEL DIARY: SICILY
Copyright © Serpent Club Press, 2025
All rights reserved

No part of this book may be used or reproduced in any manner whatsoever without written permission except in the case of brief quotations embodied in critical articles and reviews.

Serpent Club Press books may be purchased for educational, business, or sales promotional use. For more information please contact Serpent Club Press at *editor@serpentclub.org*

Second Edition
Originally published on *edahunt.substack.com*

Printed in the United States of America
Set in Williams Caslon

ISBN
9798985267624

TRAVEL DIARY: SICILY

— 1 —

EDA HUNT'S TRAVEL DIARY: SICILY

I haven't left yet, 5/4/24

I barely know where to begin, because I don't want to reveal the depths of my madness: I'm going away to the hills of Sicily for the entire summer with very little money left to my name. This was the dream I'd been holding for myself for a long time as an escape from the formless reality of, not even my life, but of life everywhere; you know, life in a godless world, trying to talk to godless people.

I'm passing the time until then by putting trim on a black felt hat, a wide-brimmed one, which is inappropriate in every way for the season, except that I am in mourning for my life. The man I love more than I thought I could, the man where all the desires of my soul and my eyes found their confluence, said he wouldn't wait for me if I went away because I wasn't promising to come back and live with him the life that he already lives.

After leaving me at the airport and three days of relentless weeping, he did contemplate washing his hands of the whole endeavor of his life in the city, leaving everything to follow me, as I have followed him the last months.

I'm torn, because I'll lose it if I yield to circumstance one more time in my life. *You're a desperado*, he said to me, *Maybe you need to go and be a desperado.*

I haven't left yet, 5/5/24

It's a dreary night where I am, and I am questioning whether I am mad. I have yet to buy a plane ticket, only the house is booked, and everyone thinks that I am mad. I'm afraid, certainly: all such quests induce such extraordinary fear, which isn't unfounded, and yet if I'm not afraid, what am I doing?

There is a big question in my life, something that has plagued my life for its entire duration, the question being why I periodically decide to face the artifically induced fear of a journey, made with a grand gesture, but more mundane fears I absolutely ignore? Mundane fears are paralyzing, but the fear of a journey is intoxicating.

I haven't left yet, 5/6/24

Why life gives us love only to take it away is beyond me. No one wants to look at their life as the open ocean, in the wake of love ending: but it is the open ocean.

I look at the lives of people I know who remain with someone they love, or used to love, in order to not ever be on the open ocean again. There must be some merit to this, otherwise people wouldn't do it. It's difficult to understand what it must be like to remain in such a situation, one that has ceased to speak to the soul but which speaks to the body and provides a structure for existence that is comfortable.

And so the end of love is rather a question of comfort versus discomfort: as the way of the layman is comfort and the way of the saint is discomfort.

Rail against it all you want, foolish woman, rail against it all you want. There is no comfort for you this morning, and there will be no comfort for you tonight in the dark as you lay, nor will there be comfort for you when you awake in the early morning before the sun, as the first birds of May have begun to sing.

In recent years, I have become very accustomed to discomfort. I learned that even when falling on your knees before God, the ground beneath you is hard and unforgiving, and the imperative to live remains. While giving myself to love, I fell back into the need for comfort, I fell back into habits of seeking it, getting it for myself, when my heart ached, knowing that I was in an impossible bind, that love could not save itself from its own demise. Left now to myself, I find that I know this place where there is no comfort and I am not afraid of it. What reason would there be to be afraid?

Modern existence has our lives revolving around comfort, and at best we are offered a set of compulsions to satisfy repeatedly throughout the days, the weeks, the years. I'm skeptical of the utility of such compulsions, I try to keep them out of my life, though I am weak sometimes.

I do not want a life that provides me a comfortable place in which to satisfy my compulsions: I've lived this already, and I left it behind for good reason. Now, on the open ocean, I see that I could make a series of choices that would lead me to slide back into such a life. I'm a woman, after all, and the world welcomes us to serve it in exchange for comfort, the world welcomes us to empty ourselves in exchange for satisfaction of some kind.

For many years, I have fought against the idea that I would have to remain alone in order to provide Life itself with a gift from my own time on earth, but I am not fighting it anymore. The more time I have spent as a good woman, the emptier I find my life to be, in great contrast to the richness of the life in my mind.

Rail against it all you want, good woman, but he has left you, and in leaving you, he has left you alone. Did you not choose solitude first? Had you been hoping that he would save you from your solitude? Naturally, you did hope for this, but sadly, you must take stock of your choices up to this point and live by them.

Individuation has no value to him, he says, he has given up: he is what he is, and it has worked for him thus far, and if it only causes me pain, there is nothing left to do. We are opposites in this way: I live by the winds of my mind, while the outer life remains neglected. This was a source of tension within our bond, the elemental tension between men and women, the external and active, versus the internal and passive; fire versus water. And the more we tried to move toward the other in that respect, the more we fought against each other. The more he needed activity, the more I needed stillness.

Are we to blame or is something else to blame? Is the upset in the natural convenience of societal roles at the root of all this? Are we victims of movements far greater than ourselves? That our lives cannot simply come together, is it a failure of love or is it a failure of the structure that is supposed to be given to love?

I haven't left yet, 5/7/24

How did so much of what we consider normal come to be normal in the first place?

Who determined that normal food is normal, who determined it to be food? I question whether most of it is food at all, if food is defined as not just edible but that it has a positive effect on the organism.

Why do we eat such complicated meals? Why do we eat three meals? Why do people expect to be entertained by what they taste?

The past week, I have eaten primarily beef tartare, because it's all I want and it's perfectly satisfying. I don't have any inclination to cook it. I've also eaten omelets, roast chicken, and a few radishes pulled from the garden. Coffee is losing its lustre, and I find that on my own, I don't want to smoke at all. Last week I didn't have a single cigarette after smoking them throughout the day for half a year.

Normalcy is dependent on context, and normalcy is also a shorthand for knowing what is considered right. It is certainly a deviation from normalcy to only eat beef tartare for a week, but perhaps my body considers normal what society doesn't. The body seems to prefer simplicity.

To go away is to get away from normalcy, to be able to question it. Remaining *in situ*, in a known context, makes it nearly impossible to change, for the norms are too entrenched and do not want to be upset.

I haven't left yet, 5/8/24

Every life has within it a central theme that plays out. In mine it is the theme of self-loathing.

If we allow it, the theme comes to us in the most terrible way, and can shatter the whole being. Or, one is already shattered within and skirts around it throughout life. Around it, and yet obsessively engaged with it. What I don't know is whether this is what makes some lives extraordinary and others sad: it might be the same act, but with different approaches.

It has been three days since I last slept, two nights behind me with only the most cursory rest. The first night, I was writing an addendum to a farewell letter to the man I love. The second night, I spent in bitter agony. The bitter agony continued through the morning, into the afternoon, and only now in the evening, a beautiful evening by May standards, it has brought me to a place of revelation, and for brief moments, merciful relief.

I knew I was going to Sicily for something: I envisioned myself at peace in nature with a view of the sea. I knew I wanted to stretch, and be quiet, and cook on a wood stove, and walk down to the shop, and eat oranges. I knew I wanted to do whatever I wanted in that time. And I knew in that time that I intended to come back to myself.

What I know now is that all of those visions will come to be, but they will be laden with the burden of my self-loathing, feeling it at every moment, as I feel it at every moment now: it has come to consciousness. It destroyed a great love, and maybe it is only the destruction of a great love that can bring a person to want to be alone with the thing that destroyed it, to have a conversation with the thing for three months, in the silence of the hills, with a view of the sea.

I haven't left yet, 5/9/24

Amidst the evisceration of self that leads to the event of leaving, there is only one choice, which is to have contact with consciousness. There is an extraordinary drive to not have this contact, because it is a pain that lights up every fiber of your being. The night passes in one long, shuddering sob, interspersed with fitful dozing and fevered pacing. As the days pass, the cause slowly reveals itself, and this is perhaps the most important part of the journey: the preparation.

During the day I have begun to prepare my body, eating only meat, eggs, and fish, and going tanning to turn myself brown all over. There's not much else for me to do right now, as I didn't expect to be where I am, waiting out the month before I leave for Sicily. I expected to be in New York, dreaming about a summer in Sicily, keeping busy, arguing, and putting off this very thing, perhaps indefinitely.

Life in America has always struck me as an imitation of life in the Old World. I could remain here and eat a plain diet, and tan in a weird little booth, to imitate the effects of a life of simplicity and sunlight; as consumerism is an imitation of plenty. I could remain here and start making money again in order to buy things. But I can no longer accept this place that has made me ill in soul and body, because what we consider a normal life here is ruinous to both, and I don't understand the purpose of being here to imitate a life that is not ruinous. I want to make this grand gesture towards vitality and not try to sustain myself any longer on substitutes.

The house I'll be living in is on the edge of a forest, where I'll collect hazelnut branches from the ground to feed the wood stove for cooking, and to heat up water for the shower. The village bakery closes at 9:00 a.m., and sometimes a shepherd brings his flock down the road. If I am hungry, I can eat. If I am tired, I can sleep. If I am sore, I can stretch. If the hours are tedious, I can face them. I don't know how I'll face the hours: in fact, I'm terrified, and have no faith in myself that I'll be able to do anything with them at all. But still, I must try.

There is a growing understanding of how rampant diseases of excess are in our society of excess. What there is less understanding of is that the excess has to be removed entirely for the body to heal. By this I mean the diet and the mode of life, they must be trimmed of all ornament so that the body and mind can achieve homeostasis and not be continuously fighting against imbalance.

American normalcy is so entrenched, however, with a mode of life that revolves around money and pleasure (even in their most temperate forms), that we play a game of substitution, a black-and-white polarity of bad and not bad. A food that is bad is simulated with a food that is not bad, but the excess remains.

I haven't left yet, 5/10/24

Waking up before dawn this morning before even the birds were awake, I did not feel the usual fear that comes upon me at that hour. I did not throw the covers aside and jump out of bed, I did not cry uncontrollably; when the sun came up, I made tea and beat three eggs in a bowl with salt, poured them into the shallow skillet to cook for a few minutes, and then ate: I have passed through the critical first days of crisis. The irony is that the crisis began half a year ago, but could not break through due to the demands of remaining present in love.

Perhaps there was a degree of sabotage on the part of my own mind, prodding me ever deeper to be freed from obligations to another in order to tend to my soul.

It would not be the first time, no. In fact, you could say that of my whole adult existence, that I have freed myself of obligation time and again in order to do so.

The unendurable having been endured, I now enter into the first plateau, where waves of self-loathing come over me, or I am skewered by it when I look at something, or attempt to act, and I have to observe it. There are a surprising number of people who, when I think of them, fill me with self-loathing: but then, everything does. If I don't want to be associated with something, it fills me with self-loathing, or if I do want to be, I flee because I am filled with self-loathing. As of today, I observe this happening over and over again, constantly. And then I observe how greedily I cling to whatever momentarily frees me from it. I suppose, then, that I should be striving for neutrality; but in the meantime, I swing wildly between the two poles.

This is the theme of my life. And because of this, I can't turn away from it. I want to turn away from it, I want to distract myself, but my life has very little distraction. How much longer will I live this way, without distraction? A year? The rest of my life?

I bought tobacco a few days ago, and am back to puffing at cigarettes throughout the day, which is how I managed the crisis in the months of its being unable to move through me. There isn't any purpose to it anymore, just a matter of habit.

"All Truth passes through three stages: First, it is ridiculed. Second, it is violently opposed. Third, it is accepted as self-evident." This is how truth comes to be in the psyche: first it is held in contempt, second it is repressed, third it is accepted. And in between the second and third, there is hell, and after the third step, there is a slower-burning hell. Thus, the third step is rarely reached, let alone maintained.

American deficiency, that is what I would call the state of being that my soul, and my body, inhabit. It is the restoration of sufficiency, plenty, that soul and body seek. But this is done through simplicity, that is my current belief. I would not call it a hope, less than I would call it a belief.

I haven't left yet, 5/11/24

As I prepare myself for radical simplicity in the old stone winehouse where I'll be living, and allow the basic tasks of existence to be completed in their own time, in realizing how very little time is needed for them, I see what a show we all make of our busyness, what knots we tie for ourselves out of our own time.

I had a similar feeling several years ago when I stopped drinking, that the evenings became very long, as if I had won a lottery of time to add to my years.

There's a fog hanging over the neighborhood today, and I stepped out this morning at dawn to cut the first flush of Greek oregano, which can be repeated all summer long until the days grow too short for the plant to regenerate. Someone has to tend to this oregano, and someone will, while I am away in Sicily. It is perhaps only mothers who tend anymore, mothers and gardeners, mothers and gardeners and people who are photographed for a living, people who live by their tendency to care for something, they tend towards it, they tend it.

Such tenders are perfecters of time, for too little time leads to neglect and the death of what is in their care; too much time and they suffer from ennui which leads to neglect just the same: those who find success know how much they can manage and do it well.

In pursuit of self-restoration in the winehouse, what will I be tending to? Myself? What does that mean? Do I know how to tend to myself? I don't think that I do, though my life has been spent tending to things that belong to other people. But I know why I am going: to cease tending what is not mine, to bring a close to that chapter of existence, and not just bring a close to it but force the opening of the next one.

At the tanning salon this morning, there I was in marshmallow flip flops, tiny red goggles digging into my eyes, rosemary oil in my braids, naked, dancing in a booth full of lightbulbs to piped-in music. It seems the dance of a megalomaniac. But I know that I'm not one: for out of the depths there always comes a rush of hostility towards myself. No, I have taken the stance of the anti-egotist, the self-loather, to expect nothing good to be said in life's looking glass.

As I wrote yesterday of my swinging between the poles, the world itself is actually neutral towards us: shouldn't we seek neutrality? Extremes distort the personality.

Love has done its duty in changing the course of my life, chasing it out of the shadows: but it will take much longer than a few months on Sicily to chase the shadows away completely and learn to live on neither pole, but between them, in neutral relationship to the world, in a harmony of sorts with life.

Tonight, I woke up from a nap, disoriented by the darkness. I stepped outside to smoke, and suddenly through the wind a trumpet rang out in *Amazing Grace*. The song continued into an unfamiliar, resplendent melody before fading out into the wind. Where the song came from, I have no idea, I've never heard anyone playing the trumpet here before.

I haven't left yet, 5/12/24

The funny thing about a descent into the abyss of oneself, is the comfort of no longer having to maintain a surface structure of compensatory beliefs.

I think of the submersible, the one that imploded, how there was a collective obsession about the fear they must have been feeling in the pitch blackness of the deep ocean. I can only imagine that there at the bottom is the sort of profound bliss of knowing that the surface is so far away, returning there is only a vague hope.

We all know what is written over the gates of Hell: Abandon hope, all ye who enter here. *Lasciate ogne speranza, voi ch'intrate*.

The descent and hope, they are intertwined. The descent cannot truly be undertaken with hope of a return, only with the assumption that there is less possibility of an ascent than of abandoning the world of light.

I haven't left yet, 5/14/24

I've mastered the art of dropping out of time and society to be able to delve more deeply into my own psyche. Thus far, nothing else has been more compelling to me, mainly because I have caused myself so much trouble in my relatively young life, that I haven't had much of a choice. And as the years bear down on me, I'm not willing to compromise and bend to my own weaknesses. My weaknesses have to leave me, and for that, I have to search them out and spend time with them.

It's an aristocratic mindset, of work being below my own endeavors, but without any of the indulgence. Yet, not quite monastic, either.

With every month that passes without working, and I have gone for great stretches of time without work, and then great stretches of only working, the concept of reputation loosens its grip on me, the concept of a façade, which is being replaced by an articulation of self and assertion of self-will. This is dangerous for someone like me, born into the lower-middle-class, because without work, you go under.

I have a theory about disease which says that not only are our bodies physically overwhelmed by excess, but we are emotionally overwhelmed, being in such close proximity to other people under stringent social rules. Rampant substance abuse is the replacement for wide open space, long stretches of time, and comfort with the range of human feeling. I think that the body wails silently as it bears the weight of all this excess, of gluttony and emotion.

Yet, it is such a rare thing to be able to go mad without being taken away. The right to go mad is, ultimately, what I have devoted the last several years to. The rest of my life exists on the other side of a period of madness, and I know this, and I have built a structure for it. I don't think that this is actually strange. What is strange to me is the idea of pursuing a life that evades madness. Madness is nothing more than the unmediated experience of one's own depths.

I haven't left yet, 5/31/24

I couldn't conceive of more perfect weather: dark and gloomy, wet, making everything incredibly green and lush, a vibrancy you don't see any other time of year, and warm.

Unexpectedly, after several weeks of eating mostly meat and a few handfuls of produce from the garden, the veil of poor health that has hung over my life for the past three years lifted. I woke up the other morning, looked in the mirror, and recognized myself.

I don't think this is a coincidence, or a surprise: a situation can become intractable to the point that you've built your life around it, as I had, until that life breaks, and once everything is shattered and lying on the ground, the solution is released from the unconscious. Nothing left to lose (having lost everything already), and no one left to please, I was free to make a socially unacceptable choice, to set myself apart in an unpleasant way. I was free to grill at breakfast and boil whole chickens to share with the dog, and to watch the days tick by in leisure as I thought about why, indeed, the refigerator needs to be so big?

To think what percentage of urban life revolves around meals being complicated affairs, that we incapacitate and disfigure ourselves just to keep busy: the logic of it all has been falling apart in my mind. Really, having nothing to lose is the most edifying thing, it makes it easy to lose illusions, too.

Over those three years of not feeling like myself, and in fact through other periods of more intense illness, I had it out with God many times: why did You give me beauty only to take it away from me? Why won't You give it back? What are You trying to get out of me, putting me through all this pain, and making me lonely, making me hide away? Will I get a reward for this? And I read passages from the Book of Job many times, I wrote them out and hung them on my wall, and memorized them.

It's a matter of hours now until I leave. I spent two long weekends with my lost love, but now I am racing to finish some sewing: a blouse, two sun dresses, in-sundry bags of printed Indian cotton to organize my clothing. I'm breaking in a pair of white Keds around the house and my mother is helping me with the hemming.

We talked about when I come back in September, but by then it's all too possible that he'll be lost for good, which is why I'll be spending tomorrow night with him, my last night in America for the summer.

After all these years: the phrase that keeps coming to mind. After all these years, everything that I have done as a fact of my own nature seems to be coming to its fruition.

Next month I will be the exact age that my mother was when she gave birth to her first child, my brother: and at that same moment in life, I will be off in the hills of the Old Country, encouraging some divine spark of my own to come to Earth.

My Arbëresh grandfather left southern Italy eighty-eight years ago. I both dread and look forward to the first time I wake up in the darkness of a Sicilian night without anyone next to me. Will the moon shine through the window? Will there be frogs in the trees? What will I dream? Will I be afraid?

Sicily 6/2/24

I spent three days packing and everything fit perfectly into the big backpack I had bought, and I thought I was so clever, until I set out yesterday in New York and could barely make it down the street under the weight. Luckily, my lost love was beside me with his laundry in a wheeled suitcase, so we went into the laundromat, put his laundry in, and put all of my things for life in Sicily into the suitcase. Having carefully packed my clothing in the cotton bags I had sewn, the transfer was effortless, and beautiful. But I felt stupid, for thinking I could carry my life on my back like that, when I stand a slight five-and-a-half feet tall.

It took five trains to get to the airport in New York, the last stretch full of Saturday beach goers en route to Rockaway. My seatmate shook me awake when they brought the coffee around before we descended in Rome. The flight to Palermo seemed to be made up entirely of American retirees. And now I am on a train running east along the northern coast of Sicily. Alina, my landlady for the summer, will be picking me up at the station with her two young daughters, "and then we can jump right in the ocean."

I'm unkempt, and drowsy. It all feels mundane, which is a relief: with age, you stop expecting your fantasies to comprise your entire life. It is easier to accept that people are people, that the apartment blocks near the tracks will be run down, but the trains and stations have been modernized, there are no charming pickpockets to watch out for, the landscape is arid, the houses are stuccoed, the balconies have sheets drying on the railing, I see cypresses, olive groves, graffiti, a horse, a junkyard, a palazzo, wooden shutters, lemons, the sun, and off in the distance, the Thyrrhenian Sea, which I last swam in when I was 19 and visiting relatives in Calabria.

The further we get from Palermo, the more beautiful everything becomes. Why do people leave Paradise and come to America?

It seems that where ever people have a yard, it is intensely cultivated and planted with peppers, tomatoes, corn, citrus and olive trees. As it should be, everywhere I look that's what I think, as it should be.

Sicily 6/3/24

Here it is, the third of June, and I woke up in Sicily at half past five with a raging headache. The sky is overcast, the view of the sea obscured, the bakery is closed, the bus into town left two hours ago, and I couldn't find the village store. I only have a bowl of oranges and lemons.

My mind is still in New York. I want coffee, I want tobacco, I want noise, I want what I am accustomed to. I am resisting Sicily. And I knew I would, which is why I came here, because the question is whether I am really the person I believe myself to be when I have all the solitude, all the time, everything that I say I need, and nothing that I say I don't want.

Alina picked me up at the train station in her converted van with her daughters. German is our common language. I was able to understand the children's Russian surprisingly well, because it's simplified, and by the end of the day we were speaking a mishmash of German, Russian, Italian, and "American".

They took me to the ocean, where we swam and ate cherries they had picked somewhere. We then drove up into the hills, went to the spring to fill big jugs of water, and then they showed me around my house as night was falling. I unpacked my things, made a fire to warm some water for showering, bathed, and apparently got into bed though I was so tired I can barely remember.

It is afternoon now, and the sky has cleared to reveal the sea and the Aeolian Islands. I was laying in bed around noon trying to sleep off the headache when there was a knock at the door downstairs. I knew that it was Giro, because Alina told me she had written to him, asking if he could help me find the store. I jumped out of bed, climbed down the ladder and opened the wooden window in the ancient wooden door of the house, and there was Giro's tanned, kind face, a cigarello in the corner of his mouth.

Dictating into Google translate, he offered to take me to the store in the next village in his car, so we drove down the hill to the shop, where I picked up rice, lentils, a tub of Sicilian olives, and coffee. He pointed out the church (*chiesa* being one of the few Italian words I know) and told me there is a mass at 9:30 on Sundays. Back in the village, Giro told me that if I ever need anything to ring at his house, and he or his wife will do what they can.

I fired up the stove and cooked a risotto, with salt and olive oil that Giro had given to Alina, presumably from his own trees. There are olive trees everywhere, absolutely everywhere, in backyards, at the edge of the forest, in large sunny groves by themselves. I managed to get a few sips of coffee out of the percolator, but it didn't boil well on the stove. Regardless, my headache has begun to ease from the food and caffeine I so desperately needed.

Somewhere nearby there is a farm with roosters and sheep. At the end of the street there is the warm, pleasant smell of ungulates, and the crowing at dawn was coming from that direction. An old man drove an old tractor through the village this morning as well.

There are flies flying and ants crawling, but I keep the floor-length window open to the forest. Just out of reach is a huge elderberry tree, which is dripping with young fruit and the last of the flowers. I've been tempted to try and pick the blooms, but I would certainly fall and break a bone.

Occasionally, I burst into tears when I remember how far away I am from the man I love. But that is part of the back-and-forth within me.

I've already run through multiple gallons of water. Still, I wanted to mop the floor, and I had to wash the dishes to keep the flies away, and I had to wash myself. But now I really feel like I'm home, after a night's sleep, a hot meal, and a little tidying up.

There is no desire here that isn't immediately tested against a cost-benefit analysis, given that a cup of coffee entails firing up the stove, which burns through the supply of cut wood, and creates ash, and doesn't produce that much coffee. Food preparation is even worse because washing dishes uses up the precious water that has to be fetched from the spring, not to mention the water for cooking itself. But I was writing about this in the weeks leading up to my departure for Sicily, questioning the utility of our American busyness, our American standard of living, as it's called, and preparing myself for a life of necessity and constraint, which conversely feels like enormous freedom.

There are children downstairs. I heard them talking loudly at the window in the door, which I opened to air the lower room. Someone drove by and beeped at them to get out of the way, and then their voices faded down the road.

Sicily 6/4/24

I couldn't wake up today, I kept sleeping and sleeping, hours after the sun had risen over Sicily. I slept more than half of a day, but I had not slept properly in a week, and I had traveled many thousands of miles.

I'm totally hamstrung in Italian, but little by little, putting the pieces together. *Fuoco* (fire), *fontana* (spring), *domani* (tomorrow), *pane* (bread), *ragazzo* (boy), *Ci vediamo* (See you later). No one seems to care that I have no idea what they're saying. Giro came by with a head of lettuce and then the neighbor with her baby, and I made the baby smile by making silly faces through my wooden door window. What are words for anyway?

There is always Google translate for conversation: *I have to bring a boy here for you. - Oh, I have a boy in New York, kind of.* (Throws his hands up) *Kind of?* (Then I throw my hands up and roll my eyes) *It's complicated.*

He knows that I'm 33, so surely the village knows that I'm 33, no wedding ring, which must be very, very old to be unmarried.

I'm eating the lettuce with lemon, as instructed. I start to calculate the cost of adding the lemon rind to my compost bucket, which has to be brought to the forest, so I put the rind in my mouth. My teeth cut right through it, and it has very little bitterness, so I eat the rest. It was grown down the street from here, so naturally it's still young and soft. I eat another slice of lemon because it is so good and sweet.

I begin to contemplate remaining in Sicily for good.

In the meantime, I made a final attempt at stove-top espresso, and failing miserably, I boiled a cup of water and poured the grounds in directly. But we don't do that in America, we have twenty different machines for making coffee, and no one would ever be so barbaric as to mix grounds directly into water, even though it works perfectly fine.

After only 48 hours, mostly sleeping and cleaning up my little *rifugio*, the life and country that I knew seem impossibly far away.

A thunderstorm has blown in with the dusk, giving the lush flora of the Sicilian hills a drink. My plans to walk to the spring have been dashed and I don't have any drinking water, so no dinner for me tonight. Yesterday, I discovered a cherry tree next to the path hanging with big, red fruit, and stuffed my pockets full. It's really the cherries that I want tonight, not the water, which I don't need until the morning anyway. But I ate an orange, rind and all, as consolation.

I'm learning quickly how to conserve water: I fill a small jar, wet the bar of soap, and suds up my whole body, taking water from the jar as needed. My hair I kind of get wet, then soap up the roots with a bar of soap. I turn on the gravity shower (warm from the stove) and as quickly as possible, rinse everything off. I feel extremely clean.

You could say that simplicity is the key to human happiness. I'm not sure if it is the simplicity itself, or whether simplicity restores the link between necessity and action. What is necessary has meaning. That is a large part of the beauty of a material good carrying the mark of the human hand, the beauty of everything created when objects had purpose. In this landscape, the purpose of nature is preserved, only improved upon: nature flourishes here regardless, but men plant more olives, more cherries, more elderberries, more oranges and lemons, more apples (oh, the apple tree dripping with fruit next to the cherry tree on the path to the spring, I'm hoping that they ripen by the end of August), because these trees are necessary if the people here want fruit. And look how beautiful they are in their necessity.

Sicily 6/5/24

Ninety days seems like so little time, when I've already spent three nights here, getting acclimated to my surroundings, getting over the jet lag. I had to force myself awake at 6:00 a.m., because if I ever want to buy the village bread or take the bus into town, I'll have to be up earlier than that.

It is another overcast day, and the heavens are shrouded in mist, from just past the edge of the forest behind the house. But it wasn't misty when I woke up, in fact, I set out early for the spring to fetch water for breakfast and the sky was clear then, all the way to the Aeolian Islands. The small water jug fits in my backpack, and I took a large jug in one hand, and a water bottle in the other.

There are two kinds of paved roads in the hills here, one for cars, and one for pedestrians. The footpath winds steeply up through the village, where the homes form a wall along the road, a rooster crows from a yard, and the voices of a very old couple waft from a window hung with a beaded curtain. At the top of the incline, the path curves around into the forest, and at the corner is a mulberry tree with dark purple fruits the size of my thumb, and a ladder leaning against the branches. Unfortunately, it is in someone's garden on top of a wall, and I have no hope of ever tasting those particular mulberries. Next to it is an olive tree, and along the top of the wall, a hedge of sage that is easily five feet in height and fifteen feet in width. The forest is a hazelnut forest, and the nuts this time of year are fuzzy and green, sitting in a lacy cup on the branches. A minute further and I see the cherry tree, but sadly I've already picked everything that was easy to pick, and I don't have the courage to climb into the tree to get more. Whose tree is it? I search for whatever is left that can be reached from the road.

The forest is cool and damp from the rain last night, and I'm a little nervous, alone at this quiet hour in surroundings that are still unfamiliar, but several minutes later I am relieved by the sight of the green metal frame encasing the spring: a spigot at the bottom of a few concrete steps, over a grate with stagnant water and moss. The water that comes from this spring is cool and pure. It is good for drinking and for washing, in fact, my skin has never been so soft. I set the jugs down, open the spigot, and wander off to pick sprigs of the abundant white yarrow growing at the forest's edge.

I fail to close the lids tightly enough. The jug in the backpack slowly leaks down the back of my sweater and jeans, but I am too focused on shifting the weight of the large jug I am carrying in my hands as I make my way back up the hill towards the mulberry tree. Then down the hill through the village I go, and an old dog barks at me from behind a gate. There is the orange tree, the bus stop, Giro's house, and then I am back at my *rifugio* with enough water for the day.

There is a fire of dried eucalyptus and hazelnut branches waiting to be lit in the stove. I set to cooking right away, and for the third day in a row, I eat risotto, which tastes just as good as the other two days with olive oil and lemon. Coffee, too. There is a funny, probably dangerous water boiler, which is a metal coil on an electric cord: the coil sits in the cup of water and in a few minutes it is hot, which is far more efficient than on the stove. After cooking, I set a pot of water over the dying fire to warm for a shower. It will remain hot for several hours. The rule with all material goods here is to squeeze another use out of them, thus, the cooking fire becomes the bathing fire, and wash water can always be used to wash something even dirtier before being tossed out the window.

After breakfast I walk past the uninhabited house attached to mine, and go down the concrete steps into the forest with the empty olive tub I've filled with compost. I don't know where to throw it, the coffee grounds, olive pits and orange rinds. Someone weed-whacked around the trees and behind the houses. I notice that the gardens behind the houses are encased by a wall, and I am not sure which is mine. Eventually, I toss the compost into a mass of green, only to realize that it's a huge bed of raspberry bushes. Later, as I am looking out my window, I realize the massive flowering shrub growing up and over the wall of my yard is also a tangle of raspberry vines.

There is always another corner to sweep out and organize. This morning, it is the pile of firewood. The day only gets cooler and gloomier, so I shut the window and start up another fire to warm the room. I desperately want to go back to sleep, but I make another coffee instead.

The room gets warmer and warmer and I take out a resistance band and weights to exercise in my underwear. I take a shower with the still-warm water and Aleppo soap. I read a little bit of Whitman. I cut down a linen towel and sew a more opaque curtain for the bathroom window, which looks out directly to the street. I sit in the upper floor windowsill to break off a young elder branch to wrap around the post in the bathroom to serve as a toilet roll holder. I make another fire and cook a pot of lentils.

I'm glad the sun isn't yet shining and beckoning me to the sea. *Domani*.

Sicily 6/6/24

I imagine that this is how soldiers feel after a battle. I took the bus into town, and have returned to tell the tale.

Getting on the bus in the morning wasn't bad. Summer arrived today, pure sunshine, not a cloud in the sky. I had washed my hair properly last night, so I braided it while I drank coffee and sent pictures of the sunrise overseas. I packed my bikini and a sunhat into a tote bag, put on a dress, sunglasses, a cardigan, and a pair of heeled sandals like the nonna's wear, and walked to the bus stop, a few steps from my house, at 6:40 a.m. A woman on the third floor of the building at the corner opened her balcony doors and called down *Buongiorno* to me, which I returned. The clucking of a chicken was coming from her apartment, and from her tone of voice, she kept telling it to quiet down, but it kept clucking. When the bus came flying around the corner about ten minutes later, I nearly threw myself at it, and the driver stopped to let me on.

Non parlo Italiano, I say, but the driver knows I'm going into town, pulls out a notebook, asks if I want a *ritorno*, which I assume means return ticket and I say yes, he punches the date, calculates the cost from the stop, and charges me three euros. I take a seat with a feeling of enormous satisfaction. The hillsides, the ocean sparkling in the distance, my triumph, everything is resplendent. The ride to town is a quarter of an hour, at relatively high speed, around hairpin turn after hairpin turn, and within minutes I'm afraid I might vomit.

Eventually, we arrive in town, I dumbly wait for the driver to tell me we're there, and get off the bus with relief. My first task is to check the coordinates Alina sent me for the bus stop, which is not where I've gotten off the bus. I walk to the coordinates, and indeed there is an unmarked bus stop, and a few feet away, a sign that says something about a "scholastic route". I've been told that I have to take the 2:00 bus back with the schoolchildren, so to best of my knowledge, this is where I will need to be. Satisfied again, I wander off into town.

It is lively at this hour, before it gets hot, and the gelateria have opened all their doors and windows and are serving espresso. There appear to be five middle-aged-to-old men for every woman in Sicily, and they stand about in groups talking, some smoking, some drinking coffee, some in the sun, some in the shade. They don't seem to take much interest in anything other than each other.

I make my way to the ocean, but the beach in town doesn't interest me. I check the map and decide to walk west, eventually crossing a little bridge to a narrow, lush street with beach-side homes to the right, and the train tracks to the left. It looks familiar. Is this where Alina took me when I first arrived? The gardens, like all other gardens in Sicily, are filled with fruit trees, enormous arbors with grape vines and wisteria. Someone has even extended their arbor over the sidewalk, so that the grapes can be picked by passersby. On the other side of the street are fig trees two stories high with budding fruits. And isn't that a mulberry? Are those the mulberry trees Alina parked underneath? They are. I've found my way back to the quiet little beach she showed me, without even intending to.

It's only 8:00 a.m. and I have the shore to myself. I change into my bikini and lay on my dress. Soon, I am covered in ants, so I move down the beach to where the sand is wetter and there are fewer ants. I take a little walk to look at shells, and notice a good deal of glazed ceramic pieces washed smooth by the ocean. I come upon a thick rectangle of granite the size of my hand, and then another one, and then a smaller piece. They're very heavy, but I put them in my bag to take home as trivets for cooking pots.

Turning myself periodically to catch the light at the right angles, I sun until 11:00, when I get dressed again to go back into town to run errands. By that time, a family has arrived with an umbrella and a brown little Sicilian boy in red glasses and a dinosaur tank top.

Several shades darker and drowsy, I meander through the city, gathering the courage to go to a store. I know that my ultimate goal is the butcher shop, the one that says "Sicilian Meats" with a picture of grazing sheep, where it won't just be a checkout line, but a counter with signs I don't understand, with items that will have to be weighed. I squint into a fruit stall where there is a shelf of dried goods: *Fagioli*, like pasta fazool, bean soup, I want to buy beans, so I go in. *Per fagioli?* I say, pointing at the brown paper bags, and the woman at the counter grunts. I fill up two bags with beans, and pick out some produce while she weighs them. She prints the receipt and points to the total, thirteen euros, I pay her and say goodbye.

Drunk on another success, I go to the bank to see if I can take out cash with my American bank card. Lo and behold, I can, and I am beside myself with joy.

I go to the discount supermarket, which smells strongly of fish. I find a jar of Sicilian honey, and a bottle of Sicilian olive oil, and paper towels, and string, and a lighter, nearly everything I need. I pass the meat counter without making eye contact. Even though I don't say anything, the woman at the register senses that I am foreign and she, too, prints the receipt and points to the total. I pay her and say goodbye.

Laden with granite, several pounds of beans, a bottle of oil, produce, and more, it is still too early in the day to buy meat, so I sun for half an hour at the city beach. Then, like a pack animal, I make my way back through the city to the butcher. I don't bother to look up any meat related words, but I manage to walk out of there with a kilo of ground beef, which is too much, considering I don't have a refrigerator, but I didn't know how to say half-kilogram.

I get to the scholastic route sign a half hour early. There are some students milling about on their phones. Buses come and go, but they're much too big for the nauseating mountain route. A small bus pulls up. The driver is fit, and about my age.

I say the name of my village, but he looks blankly back. I repeat the name, and then he says *Oh!* and pronounces it properly. *English?* Yes, yes I speak English, do you? *A little bit*, he says, he can help me. He asks where I'm from, I say New York, and he smiles brightly.

He gets off his bus, makes some phone calls, talks to some other bus drivers, one of the numerous middle-aged Sicilian men gets off a bus, and the young bus driver says, *That's your driver*, and I ask where his bus is, he says *on foot*, we all laugh. They stand there talking a while, I look off to where the buses have been coming from, while we apparently are waiting for this man's bus to be brought, which will take back to my village, God willing.

The young driver turns to me. *Holiday?* Yes, I say, three months. *Alone?* Yes, alone. *Why?* It's far away from New York, I say.

Another driver pulls up and gets out of his bus, and the three of them talk. Another bus comes, a big bus, and I am told that this is my bus, which seems wrong to me, but the driver keeps calling out the name of my village. I get on the bus and look at a map, and see that my village is named after a town further up the mountain. The man who was supposed to be my driver is also on this big bus, I tap him on the arm, the young driver is standing in the doorway, they're all talking, I hear somebody say the village name, then everyone is told to disembark and we all get on the small bus the young driver first pulled up in. He is my driver, and he will take me to my village.

I want to get away is playing on the radio as we jolt around the many corners up the mountainside and I again fear that I might vomit. Miraculously, we come to the intersection I left this morning. I thank the driver and stumble off the bus into the afternoon heat. Inexplicably, my ears are ringing as I open my door with the ancient iron key, drag myself up the ladder, and drop the heavy bags on the upper floor of my *rifugio*.

In a daze, I sweep out the stove, build a new fire, and open the window wide to let the heat out. I remove the centerpiece and set the biggest pan over the flames, dump in the kilo of beef, salt it, and let it cook while I unpack. I pour water over the old coffee grounds from this morning and hook up the water boiler, which a few minutes later boils over onto the shelf. Kicking over a pot from yesterday filled with starchy water, the meat is hissing as the fire burns too hot, I frantically start peeling zucchini to go in after the beef, when I realize I didn't wash my hands after getting home. I put the cooked beef into one of my two bowls, and add oil and zucchini to the pan, which is too hot, and splatters oil everywhere. I break a cucumber in half, peel and slice it with my dirty hands into a serving bowl with some of the beef. The zucchini continue to fry and splatter. Eventually, I dump the hot zucchini over the beef and cucumbers, which is my only option.

I ate, then I made a cup of coffee, and sat down to write. I've come to terms with the fact that I'll have to mop the floor. At least I remembered to put a pot of water over the dying fire, to warm up for all of the cleaning I'll have to do. Before the sun goes down, I'll walk down to the spring for more water, and collect firewood from the forest floor behind the house.

Sicily 6/7/24

I did it, I climbed onto the guard rail, risking the ten foot drop, to get the fat, red sweet cherries, by holding onto a dead branch and walking my fingers up from the end of the lowest hanging branches to the fruits, popping them off the stems and into my pocket. It was dusk and I had run out of water, so I was rushing down to the spring before night fell, despite being exhausted from my excursion to town, and mopping the floor. I needed water to bathe, most of all.

Squatting at the spigot filling the first jug, I hear a car pull up. I'm going to have to tell them I don't speak Italian, I think, just one more time today. A woman and her son get out of the car, and almost immediately address me. *Non parlo*, I say, but the young boy asks me if I speak English. *Yes, I speak English, I'm from America, do you? Yes, at school.* He tells me he's eleven, and named Paolo. He really doesn't speak much English at all, and so they keep speaking more and more loudly at me in Italian. *Passagio*, his mother says, gesturing to the car. A ride back to the village! I jump at the chance. As she backs up the car from the spring, I understand enough, maybe because she's so loud, to know that she's making a joke about how she's just going back to the car road and that I shouldn't worry about where she's taking me.

From the intersection where the bus had dropped me earlier in the day, Paolo insists on carrying the heavy jug to my door. He pretends to kick the door in, but it's locked. I tell him to put the bottles down but he insists that I open the door. Walking into the lower room, which doesn't look like much, he spies the guitar case. His eyes widen, he grabs the case and opens it, but it's empty. I point upstairs. Paolo makes a start for the ladder, but I grab his pudgy little arm and lead him to the door. *Your mother is calling for you*, I say in English, and send him off, *buonasera, grazie mille, Paolo*.

That was yesterday, and then I barely slept, but I willed myself out of bed at quarter of six so I could go to the forest behind the house and find the place where I have to empty the solid waste compost. Without running water, the toilet is only for liquid. Solid waste is layered with hazelnut leaves and soil in a receptacle, and then it goes back to the earth. It's a clean system, without any unpleasantness, and in fact makes much more sense, as regards resources, than the modern water-based system. The place in the forest, according to Alina's map, was underneath an elderberry tree in a massive tangle of brambles, which had been cut back but had regrown. I was armed with a pair of scissors, and spent half an hour hacking away at the vines with their massive thorns. I thought of the thorn hedge around Sleeping Beauty and the blinded princes, and the onomatopoetic German word *Stachel*, as I pulled a thorn out of my knuckle.

The task accomplished, I refilled a basket of hazelnut leaves and put a thick layer at the bottom of the waste bin. Again, a German word ran through my mind, *Laub*, or foliage, and its echoes of Goethe's ode to Italy:

Kennst du das Land, wo die Zitronen blühn,
Im dunklen Laub die Gold-Orangen glühn,
Ein sanfter Wind vom blauen Himmel weht,
Die Myrte still und hoch der Lorbeer steht,
Kennst du es wohl?
Dahin! Dahin
Möcht' ich mit dir, o mein Geliebter, ziehn.

Do you know that land where the lemons bloom, amidst dark foliage golden oranges glow, a soft wind from the heavens blows, the myrtle stands still and the laurel tall, surely you know it? There! There, with you, oh my love, I want to wander.

It would seem that today, my sixth day in Sicily, I've finally overcome all of my major challenges: how to cook on the wood stove, how to talk to the neighbors, how to buy food, how to ride the bus, how to bathe, how to gather wood and fetch water, how to get to the beach, and how to manage the compost. Will the seventh day be my day of rest?

Sicily 6/8/24

The very old woman called down to me from her balcony, and like everyone else, remained unfazed by my inability to understand or respond to her. Her house is on an incline, and she seemed concerned about me carrying the water jugs, but all I could do was repeat *Si, acqua per bere*, water for drinking, and point in the direction I was going. Her pitied looks, her insistence, her gestures, implied that I should be pulling a cart. Eventually, I set the jug down, flexed my arm to show her that I'm strong enough, she smiled and I continued on my way.

Upon my return, she was downstairs holding up a plastic bag with six eggs, *per le figlie,* for the daughters, she said: she must have thought that I was Alina. What other foreign woman has ever stepped foot here? *Non ho figli*, I don't have daughters. The old woman looked at me with sorrow but went on, telling me how the daughters run up and down the street, that she herself has four daughters living down in the city, something about *problemi*, but what family doesn't have problems? I was more than happy to take the eggs to the daughters for her, whether they existed or not, and I ate half of them for dinner that night.

When people ask me why I am here, I always shrug, why not? This is paradise: the ancient house in a fecund landscape where it is impossible to tell anymore whether it was made by God or by man. Maybe I wasn't expecting the island to endear itself to me so wholly and immediately, but it has, this place, this way of life for which we were intended, as children of God, as animals of the earth.

Unfortunately, the eleven-year-old Paolo knows where I live. He showed up at the door with his phone on a red lanyard and a picture of the Virgin Mary stuck in the case. I let him in to come upstairs and see the guitar, but he also wanted to build a fire, and write in a notebook, and help me collect wood in the forest, and then he threw wood at me in the forest, and then insisted on going back upstairs, and then took my phone and wouldn't give it back, until I ordered him down the ladder and had to physically push him out the door, my notebook and good pen in his hand, *E ora di andare a casa!* I said, shaking with anger. When he came back a few hours later to ask to borrow the wagon "to transport a statue of the Virgin", I assumed he was lying but felt guilty for pushing him out the door, so I let him borrow it.

He and his sister brought the cart back unscathed, and I walked them to the intersection on their way home, just to get them to leave. Giro was outside and I went over to say hello. Don't open the door for them, *capisci?* I didn't understand. *Don't open the door for them, they take everything.*

Sicily 6/11/24

I watched the sun come up as the morning cacophony of roosters, birds and sheep began. A thick layer of cloud hung over the ocean but below the hills, giving the impression that from my window, I was looking down at the earth from an island in the heavens. Above the clouds, the sky was glowing pink, and a gentle, cool breeze was blowing into my *rifugio*.

I wanted to go to bed, but I stayed up to cook a beef stew with *Scicli* beans at the coolest part of the day, that is, starting at midnight with a cup of coffee. Cooking over a fire is all about balance: piling on wood at the beginning to get the pot to boil, steadily feeding the flame to maintain it, and then knowing when to back off and let the embers do the rest. You can't stoke a fire without getting charcoal on your dress, and if you bring wood directly from the forest into your upstairs room all the ants of the forest will come with it, and you have to wipe the fat out of your pan with a paper towel and burn it on the embers, because you don't want to throw greasy water into the yard, and the ashes can be sifted and used to scrub out pots. As we know from the Book of Leviticus, only fire can cleanse the soul, and there are many, many rules governing the use of fire.

It's a shame we don't all have wood stoves in our homes and apartments anymore. There's a great deal of waste that can be burned; think of all the cotton and paper we use to soak up our various bodily fluids. We rely on landfills and enormous amounts of water, when it's so much simpler and more sanitary to just burn it straight away.

I was in the hazelnut forest all weekend, teaching myself how to cut the young shoots and strip them with the back of the handsaw. Hazelnut sends new growth up from the ground, straight as an arrow, which makes it superb to work with. I've made hanging bags for fruit by re-purposing textiles from my luggage, and eased a whittled rod in between two ceilings beams on the lower floor to hang cooking pots from, the shiny pots I had scrubbed with ashes and brushes made of dried grass from the forest. I learned how to twist rope from cotton twine, built a rack for the firewood, and as soon as one project had finished, I had three more in mind. The weekend passed in a pleasant creative fervor.

There is great satisfaction in being able to reap from the natural plenty around me. That is the reason for all of this work going into my daily existence: I justify my own life by maintaining it. This is possible here in Sicily, where there is still a public infrastructure for living in close proximity to nature: the springs, the forest, the fruit trees by the road, the sun, the ocean, small-scale agriculture everywhere. Here, in the middle of a village, on a bus route into the city, I am entirely self-sufficient except for my food.

For food, I went into town yesterday morning. I was the only person on the bus, no one speaks more than a smattering of English here, usually none at all, but the driver wanted to chat. I've gone from not speaking a word of Italian, to being able to occasionally say something sensible, and after so many years of that wretchedly complicated language, German, Italian is beautifully elemental and monosyllabic.

To get off the bus is *scendere*: descend, decrescendo. This being my second time, I knew on the return trip to ask which bus stopped at the bigger village downhill, not my village, which no one knows, and I knew to say *Vorrei scendere qui* as we came around the last sharp turn before my stop. I was hot, tired, hungry, and laden with bags as I walked to my door, but it was pleasantly cool in the hills and I was glad to be back there, glad to make my nightly pilgrimage to the spring, glad when Giro came by with a loaf of bread that his wife had baked, glad to eat it dipped in olive oil, glad to take a cold shower, glad to be home.

Home: this feels like my home, like my life, more than anywhere I've ever been.

If only I could get my mind to catch up with my body. I may feel peace and contentment, but the blasé aspect of modernity has followed me here: checking my phone, wondering if should buy tobacco in town instead of just browsing the selection in the vending machine, thinking about what I want to eat, the flip side of the coin of justifying my existence by maintaining it. The modern version of self-justification, which is self-soothing, hedonism, justifying existence by making it feel good. I wonder if I'll ever be able to divest myself of this, or if it is simply what man has become? Will I ever get to the other side of it?

Sicily 6/12/24

It's going on noon, the weather is temperate and overcast with the sun shining through on occasion, and the village is quiet except for a car now and then. People here are very fond of their tiny, well-maintained Fiats and mini Piaggio trucks which can fit through the narrow streets and have horns that sound like they belong to a jalopy.

As I mentioned yesterday, there is a pre-industrial infrastructure here which has sustained people as long as they have inhabited this island, which has never been destroyed, which there would be no reason to dismantle: Catholicism and the cult of the Virgin, the perennial trees and food crops grown and consumed here, the towns and villages situated in the hills and the snaking footpaths connecting them, social structures and expectations.

There is no American free-for-all on Sicily. The land and water haven't been gratuitously poisoned, no one has been taken from their homes and forced to live somewhere they are not accustomed to and that their souls don't recognize, people have roles, functions and families from which they do not want or need to be liberated, and overall there is such a simple and profound basis for human existence, that a single life, my life for instance, is not so far removed from the life of any other living thing that has come and gone over the course of centuries.

If you wanted to distill the suffering of America into a few words, you could say it is the loss of scope in how we conceive of life: roughly four to five decades of adulthood to use for the ruthless acquisition of some of the plenty that was never set aside for common use; and therein lies the loss of a proper place on Earth, of a context within nature and her laws, and within a span of time that far exceeds any single existence.

I've been in a bone-deep exhaustion since yesterday. I was up at dawn, drank coffee and ate breakfast, but was overwhelmed at the thought of taking the bus down the mountain and then catching a train one town east, as was my plan. Instead, I laid down again and slept four more hours. In the afternoon, I walked to the forest spring, which is on the footpath heading north, downhill, towards the coast. There is no spigot, just pristine water flowing continuously out of a pipe sticking out of a wall over a concrete basin. I only bring the backpack jug and a water bottle to this spring, because it's quite a bit further and entirely uphill on the return. Then I collected firewood, cut and stripped a hazelnut shoot, bent it into a circle and secured it with twine: I'd like to weave a hazelnut basket.

All of my needs have been met. Now what? Do I lay down to sleep? Read? Look out at the hills and the ocean? Eat an apple? Surely there has to be an urge that comes from somewhere deeper, for a serious undertaking, but I cannot find it.

I am downstairs washing my hands when I hear a whistle at the window. It's Giro. *Come stai? Bene, stanco.* I mime sleeping, and he corrects my Italian: *stanca,* because I'm a woman, I think. I ask him *Come stai,* he responds *cosi, cosi; domani, tempo, arance,* he's alright, and something about tomorrow, time and oranges. I go upstairs and get my phone to translate. It turns out that he wants to tell me that if he has time tomorrow, he'll pick me some oranges. I ask where his garden is and he points down the road, the same direction I went in this morning to go to the forest spring, and we make a plan to go there tomorrow at 3:00 after I've gotten back from town. He comes back a little while later with two onions fresh out of the ground, and the only word I understand is *pomodori,* tomatoes.

The naivete of youth has left me. To be the *belissima ragazza* in the village for the summer is worth its weight in citrus, but to be loved is not the same as to love.

Sicily 6/13/24

I love being a woman in Sicily. It is the most natural thing in the world, wearing a skirt, and shoes that lift your heels, and being treated with reverence. When the bus gets into town at 7:20 there aren't any other women about, only the men drinking espresso.

The women come out when the shops open a little later. I wore a long orange skirt and a yellow shirt, but the women here dress like birds of paradise, and I am no anomaly. Except that I sinned greatly, in my rush this morning, in not putting on a bra, which is not acceptable here. A man even cleared his throat as he passed me. But it was too late, of course, once I realized what I had done.

I had to take the train one stop east to a bigger town today to get a metal bucket for the stove ash. It's a resort town, where I came across fellow Americans for the first time today, a chubby family in summer-wear at the train station. I ran quickly past them.

Most of the day was just killing time waiting for trains and buses: looking out at the ocean, answering a backlog of texts and emails, walking and walking, buying and eating *frutta*. I got the bucket I needed, with great rejoicing.

My ear has grasped the swing of Italian enough that I am not shocked by it anymore. When I got back to my town, I went to the butcher shop, the site of my disgrace, and with great confidence announced *Vorrei und bisteccha, per favore,* and the woman got a slab of meat, cut a piece, said *Una?*, I said *Due*, and I paid less than five euros.

I think I'm in love with Sicily.

Ever the adventure, today the bus drivers told me to get on the big bus, one of the big buses that would never, ever, make it around even one of the sharp turns up the mountain. Incredulously, I repeated the name of the village route. No, no, it's definitely the big bus, just get on the big bus, they all insisted. So I got on the big bus, alone.

For some reason, I really trust the Sicilians, that they have my best interest in mind.

All was well until the bus took the wrong exit. Where was it taking me? How would I get back to my village? A minute later, we pulled into the bus depot. *Camminando, altro autobus.* I've understood that we have to walk to another bus. So we get off the big bus and walk to one of the small buses, the driver starts the bus, says something, and then we get off and walk to a different small bus, then, he gets off the bus and goes and puts something in his car, then we pull out to leave the bus depot, but then he gets off again and says something about *tempo*, which from the context I think means he'll be right back, and then we're off into the hills, which never fails to nauseate me. Giro is sitting in his garage when I get off the bus at the village, and I greet him, miming that I am sick to my stomach from the turns.

We don't realize how short life is until we start living it again, or that we have treated it as something less than sacred. Which is maybe Sicily's greatest gift to me, to remind me that life has come from somewhere far beyond my grasp. That I am here at all.

To remind me that at dawn the animals call out to the heavens, and that I am no different from them.

Someone has harvested and pruned back the sweet cherry tree, and the only fruit left is being eaten at by bugs. The time to harvest is brief. I was on my way to the spring with the wagon for the first time, pulling five jugs with me since I have laundry and dishes to do. I'm not sure why I resisted taking the cart for two weeks, it's not fun on the way back with all that water, but no worse than carrying it by hand.

The dusk tonight took my breath away. The warm glow of the streetlights in the villages nestled into the black hills, against the pastel sky, which melds into the ocean, in the distance a few lights glowing on the islands. I stood in my windowsill watching the day fade, listening to the rustling leaves of the forest and the now familiar voices of the family across the way from me.

Sicily 6/14/24

There is a natural inclination in people towards doing what is easiest. Unless we are given no choice but the difficult route, we won't take it, or at least it's very hard to find and then maintain the motivation. And even then, I suspect that when the motivation is found, it comes from some threshold having been crossed, in which the difficult route has become an imperative on some level.

I appreciate this about my life here, that I have no choice but to walk a mile round trip for water, and I have no choice but to collect wood and build a fire if I want to eat, and I have no choice but to learn Italian if I want to communicate. The irony is that none of this feels difficult: it just is. When the sun is shining over the cerulean sea and the stuccoed villages reflect the light along the ridges of the hills, the air smells of linden and yarrow, and I'm eating a tart, half-ripe apple from the roadside, what do I care that I'm pulling a heavy cart of water jugs?

The door window is open downstairs for the laundry drying on a line strung across the room. A whistle, and there is Giro, he has a cucumber for me, the first one of the season. *Non losere,* he says, don't lose it, pointing to my shorts. Of course, I don't have any idea what he's saying, but he's long gone by the time I translate the joke. The Sicilians are endearing themselves greatly to me with their straightforward natures, and lack of shame.

Early evening, cooking while it's hot out to see if the heat dissipates by nightfall, and it's not as bad as I thought it would be. I've been strategic: first the *bisteccha*, which needs the least amount of time, then the oatmeal for tomorrow, and lastly the bean soup, which requires the most heat (when the stove is filled with hot embers) for the greatest length of time (after cooking it can sit on the warm stove for the rest of the night). Perhaps a metaphor for life, the hardest part that requires the most attention, is getting that last big pot to boil; once it is boiling, it is difficult to get it to stop.

The last two weeks, simply having no concept of a routine with cooking over fire and not having a refrigerator or easy access to a store, I was eating great amounts of food out of a strange scarcity complex as soon as I was done cooking. I think that is ending, though, and I look forward to getting more figs (figs the size of tennis balls) in town on Monday, on my way to the beach.

I am wondering how much of life flows from what we believe we exist for? I exist to...could have any myriad endings, and let's say there are five that form the basis of the majority of my actions. You see, because I did away with some of the more damning beliefs about my existence, I find myself doing alright, but now I am here in this *rifugio*, and I find that what I *want* to exist for does not align with what I *do* exist for, the latter being a sort of not-destructive version of the old belief system. More than anything, I'm annoyed, that a change of place hasn't magically activated a new way of being, although it is doing me a world of good to be here. The ultimate good, however, will be a conscious activation of a new way forward, and a letting go of the desire for magic.

The *lozione schiarente* I bought has made me a strawberry blonde of sorts, their proprietary chamomile extract with just a hint of hydrogen peroxide. It's the sort of thing you find in a foreign supermarket on the edge of town past all of the auto dealers, when you're the only person who's gone there on foot and life wants to reward you for your efforts.

Sicily 6/16/24

I've had my first bad day here, not that anything bad happened, only the tragedy of acclimation. Since Thursday afternoon I've been up in the hills, and since last night there have been rally cars racing through the area, though I don't know why. Paolo knocked at my door to invite me to watch them, but I gave a stern *Non mi piace*, and it was Giro's invitation to sit at the intersection with some other neighbors and watch them go by, again and again, that got me outside. He gave me a basket of oranges yesterday at his *orto*, where he and his wife were also pruning the orange tree, and some zucchini and cucumber, so I couldn't say no. But I was in a terrible mood to begin with, there's nothing more boring to me than cars, and the relentless noise all across the valley has been driving me up the wall.

Why is acclimation a tragedy? The return of the mundane.

A long, distressing dream, about over-promising and not having enough resources, woke me at 3:00 a.m. To distract myself from the unconscious, I decided to light the fire in the stove and cook the pot of beans and rice I had soaking in the big pot. I got the fire started on the first try and fed it steadily until a remarkably hot bed of embers had formed. Still, it was 5:00 a.m. before I salted the pot, stirred it, put in the last of the wood, and went back to sleep while the beans finished cooking. When I got out of bed three hours later, the ashes were cooling and I had a warm breakfast ready.

I think that some of the pain of what I am calling mundanity, is lack of familiarity with a less regulated flow of time. I am accustomed to regulating time with stimulants, screens, people, acquisition, and busyness. Subsisting largely on beans and rice, salt and olive oil, often forgetting to make coffee until an hour into the morning, having made it two weeks without nicotine, having grown used to cold sponge baths, firewood and forest springs, the burden of challenge here has shifted from activity back to thought. As time-regulating activity fades away because there is no real purpose to it up here in the village, and indeed my goal is for it to fade away, life seems terribly mundane, because I don't, in fact, really know what to do without it.

So I writhe, and mope, and lay on the bed trying to nap, and read old message threads, and eat some beans out of the pot, angrily pine over my lost love, and drag myself to the spring though I don't need water tonight, but strangely, none of it is genuinely attached to desire for anything. I don't want any of what I don't have. I want that indefinable other thing, which exists somewhere underneath the petty, actually mundane habits of the American city dweller.

At the very least, being here in Sicily takes away the question of why I exist, why life exists, being surrounded by so many living things in harmony with their environment: life exists in order to express the harmony of existence. It's a different question that plagues me, which is what to do. Why don't I have an answer to this? Why am I so determined, why have I come all this way, to look for an answer to this?

Thank God, the rally cars have stopped as the sun sets, peace has returned to the hills and the only sound is the rustling elderberry tree.

Sicily 6/18/24

Just when I thought the adventure had petered out, fate stepped in.

For the second day in a row, I was at the intersection at 6:30 in the morning, reading *Leaves of Grass* on the bench and waiting for the bus. It didn't come yesterday, and by 7:30 this morning, it still hadn't come.

Giro came down, as usual in a polo shirt, shorts and flip flops, and opened his garage. It's hard to tell if anyone works in Sicily, if they do, they certainly don't seem to have any stress in their lives. Giro is retired from what I can tell. *Non é passato*, I complain. *Aspetta,* he says and points to the curb outside of his house. I look up what that means and then complain further, *Aspetto un'ora...* but he insists, and I gather that he's going to try and flag someone down to give me a lift.

To my great delight, he snags a red Fiat Panda from the eighties, driven by a bookish young man with glasses and braces. He waves me into the passenger seat and I get in. His English is as good as my Italian, so we don't say much, and next thing you know, he's dropping me in the *città*. The interior of the car is indescribably beautiful to me, so mechanical, so well-maintained, it even has a panel of padded seersucker on the dashboard, and manual window rollers. This is what I came here for, I think. My dreams are coming true.

The store with the giant figs is open and I go there first. I've learned not to touch the produce here, someone will get it for you, so when I spot those five enormous figs I declare *Tutti i fichi*, all of the figs, *per favore*. It doesn't matter what I buy here, I can't seem to spend my money, and I know these figs are going to cost me next to nothing. I carry on, buy some grapes, and then go to my favorite beach, the one by the mulberry tree that has chunks of granite in the sand.

It's still early when I arrive, only 8:30 in the morning, and I have the beach to myself. I lay in the sun, wade out into the water which is demonstrably warmer than it was only two weeks ago, dip once, dip twice, lay in the sun and eat figs and grapes, go back in the water, and by 11:45 I have to drag myself away from this little paradise to do more shopping before everything closes at 1:00 for the afternoon. By then, a good wind has picked up and made the clear, calm blue sea a little choppy.

By the time I get to the bus stop, I'm carrying pounds of produce, pounds of dried beans, an enormous steak, a kilo of ground beef (because I still don't know how to say half-kilo), several pieces of beach granite, a bottle of olive oil (my third in two weeks), a jar of honey, paper towels and toilet paper, but the park is awfully quiet, and there isn't a single bus here yet. I wait a little, and then I notice a sign posted to the otherwise unmarked bus stop:

DAL 17 GIUGNO AL 7 SETTEMBRE LE LINEE—oh yes there's my bus route!—*SARANNO SOSPESO*. I look it up: will be suspended. Suspended? There's no bus into town until September? I text Giro, who says his son-in-law can be there in a few minutes. He's on his way home from work driving through town, and I recognize him as the man who stopped by Giro's apartment this morning while I was waiting for the bus. What luck.

New York is great! he says, when I tell him where I'm from. I disagree. But why Sicily, why have you come here? Oh, to get away from New York, *io è mio ragazzo, basta*. *Ah, but the Sicilian men!* he says. And we do agree that Sicily itself is beautiful. The sun is shining and all of these nice people are driving me around. I feel so happy, and then we're pulling up in front of my little stone house. *Grazie, grazie, grazie!* I say, and he responds *Prego, prego, prego!* I set my bags down upstairs and break out into laughter, at life.

And that's what I mean about fate stepping in. What I really want is to have to hike up and down the mountain to get to the beach. What I really want is absolute independence, to come and go from my *rifugio* as I please. These villages were built long, long before cars, and I'm certainly not the first person to look at the deep blue sea and feel a great determination to walk towards it. I can't tell you, the levity I feel tonight due to what, at the bus stop this afternoon, seemed like my undoing.

In the evening, I want nothing more than to take a shower, but I have no water left. I have to go to the spring. My skull is being crushed by another migraine. The old lady with the eggs is standing in the street with another, younger woman, watching me come down the steep hill backwards, below the cart. They want to chat and, like everyone else in Sicily, they want to know if I'm *sposata*, married. *You don't do this in New York!* they say, laughing, pointing at the cart.

Yesterday, when the bus didn't come, I dejectedly went back to my house, got the bar of Marseilles soap and washboard, sat on the stone floor, and washed my towels. Rinsed them, wrung them out, hung them to dry. Picked up the handsaw and went to work on the wood stacked against the wall. To my surprise, the handsaw made quick work of it; much more efficient than scrounging for deadwood on the forest floor that is small enough to break. I let run a few tears for my lost love, who is much on my mind lately. Like a bramble thorn, the puncture wound left behind is more painful than the thorn itself.

But that was yesterday, at the end of my weekend, when I had no wind in my sails and no adventure in my heart. Today is different. Perhaps the adventure is just starting today.

Sicily 6/19/24

Absolute value: a foreign concept to this traveler from the brave new world.

My chosen circumstances force me to consider the true value of things. How far am I willing to walk, how much weight am I willing to carry, how much wood am I willing to saw through and burn, how many thorns am I willing to get stuck with, how much of the unknown am I willing to face, to get it?

Meat and ripe fruit inspire quasi-devotional thinking. Rice with zucchini disappoints entirely when you calculate the labor invested in the fire. A raging headache is meaningless when you need water to wash your hair and dusty feet before bed.

None of this is a matter of personal preference, rather, it is an expression of our natural reward system, in place for the proper delegation of one's energy. I can see how determined and inventive I am in this environment, where the rewards are good for me, and the byproducts of my efforts are good for me. It changes my thinking on having gone into recovery, that is, having had the humility and courage, to admit that my life had come to revolve around a specific and destructive reward: perhaps I was in an environment where the given rewards had no purchase with me, no meaning, and so I chose something more immediate, with destructive rewards that I was nonetheless willing to suffer for.

We know this, of course, we all know that our entire society suffers from a perversion of the evolutionary effort-reward feedback loop, because nothing requires effort and we have access to limitless reward. When I was daydreaming about fasting and sunbathing and the ocean, what made me think not even twice before renting my now-beloved *rifugio*, was that somewhere not terribly deep down, I knew I would never be able to move beyond the fallacious pleasures of the New World unless I left it behind for a time.

The sweet odor of burning cherry wood wafts into my room as I make a pot of Scicli beans shortly after sunrise. Cherry is the hardest wood to saw through, but the scent makes it worthwhile.

There is a greater sense of urgency with cleanliness here. Not only because water is so hard to come by, but because you sweat through all of your clothes, flies will come and make an unholy racket over crumbs, and you'll find ants in jars that aren't hung up on the wall. I am always sweeping, washing, wiping, and burning away the traces of my existence so that I may continue to exist in peace.

It's a matter of arranging, and balancing. Arranging resources and balancing needs in a subtle dynamic that solves problems when they are small. (Why collect and aggregate problems and try to solve them on a bigger scale?)

Man is not actually the pleasure-seeking monster modern life has made him out to be. Man is actually quite reasonable, quite savvy, when reason and savvy are rewarded.

Sicily 6/20/24

My intention was to take the forest path to the next village, except the dog was there again. When I first encountered it, with its owner, it tucked tail and ran off from me down the hill. But this time, it was alone and sitting about twenty feet off the road, some kind of mutt with German Shepherd in it.

The path goes through a large farm, with chickens, roosters, goats, countless olive and fruit trees, and terraced gardens. The owner is a very old, stooped woman, at least that's who was with the dog last time. She spoke to me but I couldn't understand her.

I turned around and went back through the forest, past my house, and got onto the *strada provinciale* that snakes its way down the mountain. Just as I was exiting the next village, which I look at every night and every morning from my window, a single road along a mountain ridge with a church at the end, a car pulls up. It's none other than Giro, of course, with his wife, and a daughter, a granddaughter, and a niece in the back seat. There isn't any room for me, but his wife, who isn't a small woman, shifts into the middle of the front seat and insists that I squish myself in next to her, which I do, of course.

Once in town, I buy fruit and go to the beach, where I lay in the sun, make some acquaintances, and dip in the water, for the next four hours.

Home is 5.4 miles and 2000 feet in elevation from where I am sitting at sea level. There is no bus, I'm not going to hitch-hike, nor ask anyone for help. It's mid-afternoon, 90°F and I think that I'll be just fine with 20 slices of bresaola, and no water.

I'm writing this from my *rifugio*, so you know that I made it home. My only regret was taking a shortcut through an olive grove which turned out to be incredibly steep and went on for a good twenty minutes before I could get back on the road, my heart pounding. As I came down the hill into my village, I was smiling irrepressibly. The back of my dress was soaked through and my face was bright red from the exertion, but I had made it.

It reminded me of hikes in the Alps when I was younger, where, at the end of the day you look down into the valley you started from and can't quite believe that you got up so high on your own two feet.

Sicily 6/26/24

My ankle is all torn up. Not from the dogs, luckily, but from the thorn bush I jumped into to get away from them. The same dogs at the same intersection in the lower village, alerted by the other dog behind the fence.

At first, I thought they would stay back and just bark at me from their garage, but no, they're trotting up the hill towards me, barking and barking. Where do I go? To the side of the road, and I look down into an olive grove, it's a drop. Would they jump after me? How would I get out of there? So I jump up, onto the low retaining wall, and walk as quickly as I can without falling. A red car up ahead has stopped, and the driver is talking to the driver of a stopped car going in the opposite direction. As I pass, shaken up, she calls me to her window.

I think my days of walking to town are over. It's so far, and there's no way around those bastard dogs.

Am I the only person who ever goes on foot here? How can these dogs just terrorize this intersection? Is it because they can smell my fear?

The woman gives me a ride to my village. At the intersection, she says, *Giro is your neighbor?* Small world, she knows Giro, she honks her horn, I hear a whistle come from the forest. He appears, his wife comes out on the balcony, and the woman in the red car tells them the story. Oftentimes I hear a conversation here that sounds like a fight, and then everyone will suddenly say *Ciao* and part ways, friendly. It was like that, the way she told the story.

What I can understand is that they're talking about how it's so far, the dogs, *she says she likes walking!, she always wants to go to the beach!,* how could my friends go to Germany for the summer and leave me here like this, I need a car, and so on. They say it's a *bordello*, a real mess. When she leaves I say to Giro, *She seems really upset*, and he says, *She was just scared*. I'm embarrassed to put all these people out, who are so kind to me. That's when he points at my ankle and I see that I'm bleeding quite a lot. I hadn't noticed.

I had spent the day one town over. One of my former bus drivers saw me walking around, honked at me and waved. I waved back but I wanted to stop him and say, *You abandoned me!*

On my way back, hot and tired, dejected because my bermuda shorts made me invisible to men all day, I'm pacing the platform when a slick, silver fox type asks me a question about the train as an opener. His English is good, but halfway unintelligible. I'm from New York, he's the captain of a super yacht on his way back to Palermo with his teenage son, and his parents are flower exporters. *Do you want a smoke?* he says, and I respond *Oh, yes!* as my last one was on this very platform, when I arrived here twenty-five days ago.

He gives me his number, tells me to call him next time I'm in Napoli, and as my train pulls up, grabs my face and kisses me on the cheek.

I had just answered an email from a recording studio in Brooklyn. The schedule's filling up, do I want to book? I ask about September, while my guitar has been gathering dust up in the mountains.

I had just come out of a church where I anointed myself with holy water and sat for a long time, praying with my eyes glued to a mosaic of Jesus.

Now it's the middle of the night at *rifugio*, I'm drinking coffee, eating steak, cooking, and intending to stay up until I figure out how to get to the beach despite the dogs, without having to depend on the good will of Giro for the rest of the summer. Out of drinking water and desperately thirsty, it's another four hours until sunrise.

There's a path through the forest that Alina sent me a map for, or I could get really good at hitchhiking. How was I supposed to know? All of those nightmares about being chased by dogs had to come to life.

Sicily 6/24/24

The Tyrrhenian Sea yesterday was the most beautiful sea I have ever seen. From up here in the mountains, it was an impossible color. I was reminded of a line from a poem written on the Baltic many years ago: *I've spent many days now sitting on shore / And still have no name for this blue.*

I think that we gravitate towards the ocean when something has gone wrong within us, or within our lives, the ocean being unconquerable by man and bearing the rhythm of the cosmos or of the wind. It is reassuring, listening to the beating heart of the world, as if you had laid your head on its chest.

Although today I have to fetch water and collect and cut wood and later on use a lot of it to cook, I've gotten dressed. My hair is braided, my linen shirt is tucked in with a leather belt, and my nails are trimmed and filed. The old women here wear a dress to sweep off their porches, and the old men wear button-downs and suspenders to tend to their olive trees in the morning.

As much as I enjoy being a woman in town, up in the village I enjoy being a person with work to do.

The younger generations, particularly the teens mimicking Americans, are more casual, but generally people will be as proper as their surroundings. That many of the houses here are refurbished and inhabited in stages, leaving entire facades as bare terracotta block until they can get to stuccoing them, or with a crumbling stone hut attached to the side, has nothing to do with slovenliness. It is only that here the centuries are layered on top of one another, and there is no shame in using what you need, and leaving what you do not need in memorandum.

Quiet dignity, purposive action, dry air, salt water to bathe in, spring water to drink, green hills to walk, and a view of the horizon. I knew what it was I needed, when I was suffering in New York all fall and winter. There are no mistakes: when called, go.

In short, the antidotes to the city: its indignity (streets piled with garbage, rats crossing your path, schizophrenics and addicts on corners and subway cars), that action is dependent and mediated (having first to be transformed into money, ingoing and outgoing), that the heat is wet, that the Atlantic is salty but a dirty green and the state of the beach-goers reflective of hedonistic lives lived in theory, that the drinking water is poisoned, that there are flat, dirty parks that reek of marijuana instead of hills, and assuredly no view of any horizon, without or within.

What changes in an environment of the former, is a return to inwardly-held dignity, which is not easy. The longer one has been sapped of it, the more grotesque and misshapen the physical posture and the mental and emotional attitudes, and these take time to release, that is, if you can first overcome the distress of recognizing this at all.

I'm not sure if there's anything worse for a human being than to be stripped of their dignity, or held a few rungs below it. It turns the heart bitter and gives the capacity to destroy.

My arch nemesis today is the cherry wood. It takes 200 strokes to get through a branch half the size of a piece of hazelnut which only takes 50 strokes to cut through. Why don't I throw it back into the forest? Because I want to maintain my composure, develop patience and perseverance, in the face of a task that is harder than I want it to be. Furthermore, the same could be said about this entire endeavor, that humanity has already learned how to not do any of this, how to not cut wood at all to cook food. There are arguments on both sides, that working harder to get what you need keeps you fitter and healthier, makes it more difficult to indulge or squander, and yet, if the practical side of life is easier then you're free to tend to higher undertakings. And yet, what have we learned about human nature in our age? What have we learned about our self-conceits?

The world of today turns us against ourselves: that's what we've learned. The world used to be against us, we used to have to fight it, but now we've taught it to coddle us, and by and large that's to our detriment. There is an inward collapse.

I don't say this to disparage anyone's attempt to make a good life for themselves and their family in the world as it is given to them. I'm writing, rather, as someone who took the world personally and carried it on her shoulders, and it's a relief to understand (through action, in Sicily), that it was the world all along.

I've discovered a correlation between the stove handle being too hot to touch and the beans finally coming to a boil. Two hours after I started the fire, I'm sitting down to eat them, Scicli beans with brown rice and celery root. The good news is that I really didn't go through that much wood. Since I started sawing down bigger branches, even whole saplings, it burns much slower and I only have to feed the stove every twenty minutes or so. That said, it easily takes an entire sapling to cook a pot of beans, a dead sapling dragged out of the forest.

Everything closes and the streets are empty in the afternoon. The day is starting to cool down as people trickle outside for the evening. I've just emerged from the dappled hazelnut grove with an armful of wood.

Sicily 6/25/24

It rains in my heart as it rains on the town. A warm summer rain is falling over the sleeping north coast of Sicily, perhaps the whole island, but how am I to know?

I started a fire and had an idea, a predawn hour idea: if I cook a small pot of rice while the embers develop and the stove warms, I can set the pot of beans next to it on the stove top to start warming up. Indeed, the rice cooked and the water in the bean pot started to warm, all at once. Do you have any idea how much wood this saves? Are you also asking yourself why it took me twenty-five days to come upon this? Although rice hardly inspires the same fervor that slow-cooked beans do, it cooks quickly over a new fire and takes my mind off of eating for a couple of hours.

This being the first real rain of my summer here, it seems monumental, that it is washing away the past.

I am reminded, too, of my upbringing in the humid mid-Atlantic, where it can thunderstorm every night for stretches in the summer. My family, across the ocean, seem more present while it rains than they ever do while the sun in shining.

But where is home anymore, now that I have been to Sicily?

The songbirds and roosters have begun to sing and to call, as the rain ceases to fall and settles into a mist in the valleys. My little room is warm from the stove, and I stopped trying to give up coffee, because it is so pleasant here to drink coffee in the morning. I've decided against going into town, when it is so cool in the hills and I have a stack of wood from the forest that has to be cut. Furthermore, my pin curls are still damp from the humidity, so I might as well let them set until tomorrow.

A simple life is a pleasant life, with simple and pleasant decisions.

While this could never be recreated in America, due to the lack of human-scale interconnection—such that the village houses form the street and the neighbors do not have to approach your door, the center of commerce is reachable by foot if you are young and healthy, the environment is pure with public access to water and wood—I'm dreaming of building a summer home. People have always fled the cities for the summer if they could, to be in a purer, cooler place with sunshine, little overhead, and no connection to the vanities and pains of winter in the metropolis. Americans build cabins in the forest, but I assure you, a village is a better and happier place than the wilderness, to me.

The advent of the American suburb collapsed seasons and different modes of being into one, and stripped the agricultural element from the green space surrounding each family's home, particularly perennials and animal husbandry; the former being heritable and the latter providing dense nutrition.

I don't have any adventures to write about with so many days on end at the *rifugio*.

We are so captivated by and entangled in our subjective consciousness that we have forgotten the age-old fact that God speaks chiefly through dreams and visions, said Jung.

You could say I had my visions of this place before I ever came here, and the visions came in the form of questions that needed to be answered, and the need for the answers led me to the place where I thought they could be.

Why don't I want to live the life that I have? Why is my body suffering? Why has a mutually experienced love gone up in flames? Why am I a stranger in the land of my birth?

Sicily 6/26/24

My ankle is all torn up. Not from the dogs, luckily, but from the thorn bush I jumped into to get away from them. The same dogs at the same intersection in the lower village, alerted by the other dog behind the fence.

At first, I thought they would stay back and just bark at me from their garage, but no, they're trotting up the hill towards me, barking and barking. Where do I go? To the side of the road, and I look down into an olive grove, it's a drop. Would they jump after me? How would I get out of there? So I jump up, onto the low retaining wall, and walk as quickly as I can without falling. A red car up ahead has stopped, and the driver is talking to the driver of a stopped car going in the opposite direction. As I pass, shaken up, she calls me to her window.

I think my days of walking to town are over. It's so far, and there's no way around those bastard dogs.

Am I the only person who ever goes on foot here? How can these dogs just terrorize this intersection? Is it because they can smell my fear?

The woman gives me a ride to my village. At the intersection, she says, *Giro is your neighbor?* Small world, she knows Giro, she honks her horn, I hear a whistle come from the forest. He appears, his wife comes out on the balcony, and the woman in the red car tells them the story. Oftentimes I hear a conversation here that sounds like a fight, and then everyone will suddenly say *Ciao* and part ways, friendly. It was like that, the way she told the story.

What I can understand is that they're talking about how it's so far, the dogs, *she says she likes walking!, she always wants to go to the beach!,* how could my friends go to Germany for the summer and leave me here like this, I need a car, and so on. They say it's a *bordello*, a real mess. When she leaves I say to Giro, *She seems really upset*, and he says, *She was just scared*. I'm embarrassed to put all these people out, who are so kind to me. That's when he points at my ankle and I see that I'm bleeding quite a lot. I hadn't noticed.

I had spent the day one town over. One of my former bus drivers saw me walking around, honked at me and waved. I waved back but I wanted to stop him and say, *You abandoned me!*

On my way back, hot and tired, dejected because my bermuda shorts made me invisible to men all day, I'm pacing the platform when a slick, silver fox type asks me a question about the train as an opener. His English is good, but halfway unintelligible. I'm from New York, he's the captain of a super yacht on his way back to Palermo with his teenage son, and his parents are flower exporters. *Do you want a smoke?* he says, and I respond *Oh, yes!* as my last one was on this very platform, when I arrived here twenty-five days ago.

He gives me his number, tells me to call him next time I'm in Napoli, and as my train pulls up, grabs my face and kisses me on the cheek.

I had just answered an email from a recording studio in Brooklyn. The schedule's filling up, do I want to book? I ask about September, while my guitar has been gathering dust up in the mountains.

I had just come out of a church where I anointed myself with holy water and sat for a long time, praying with my eyes glued to a mosaic of Jesus.

Now it's the middle of the night at *rifugio*, I'm drinking coffee, eating steak, cooking, and intending to stay up until I figure out how to get to the beach despite the dogs, without having to depend on the good will of Giro for the rest of the summer. Out of drinking water and desperately thirsty, it's another four hours until sunrise.

There's a path through the forest that Alina sent me a map for, or I could get really good at hitchhiking. How was I supposed to know? All of those nightmares about being chased by dogs had to come to life.

Sicily 6/27/24

I have a theory that the draw of checking our phones is connected to the deep desire for the divine to answer us. We are enchanted by the idea that we can speak to someone who is not physically present. I am not sure if dopamine plays as big a role in telephone dependence as we think it does. It's rather that it takes away the pain of God never answering, and this is particularly true of social media, where we are hearing from people we admire. No one is enjoying themselves when they keep refreshing the same things all day, every day; there's something else that it's doing for them.

I started taking the pull cart to the spring in the forest. The long hill on the return trip makes my calves burn wildly, and I'll never again attempt fifty liters like I did the first time. Usually I go in the evening, but I hadn't slept and I desperately needed water. Mornings are a busy time in Sicily, everyone trying to get a little bit done while it's still cool. An old couple driving through the forest to the farm down the road stopped twice, there and back, to chat with me. *Why did you leave your door open?* he said, this villager I'm not sure I've ever met before. My door was just barely ajar, there's no point in locking it, but he noticed.

There is an enormous fig tree, two or three stories tall, that I pass just past my house. The fruit is beginning to ripen. I snuck one the other day; it had a purple and white interior and tasted like pure sugar. I'd been eyeing up another one that looked ready to go, but I knew it had to belong to the big, beautiful house with the opulent garden across the street.

On my way back from the spring, an old couple was outside working. She was sweeping and felt bad that I had to haul water, but I reassured her. As I approached the man at the fig tree, I noticed his body was very stiff and he couldn't move well. He slowly reached out his hand to me: in it was the fig I wanted.

In the afternoon, sunning with a book on my wide stone windowsill, hidden by the elder tree, I hear Giro's daughter passing by with the baby carriage. Her daughter has enormous brown eyes, and she is singing *Pretty girl! Pretty girl! Pretty girl!* to the baby. She is the happiest, most content mother I have ever seen. We're probably the same age, but there is no gulf between us as a mother and a not-mother.

What I've learned over the last ten days of there being no bus into town, is that you shouldn't seize too greedily upon opportunities to make life hard for yourself in the hope of forcing a change to come about. If other people are having to get involved just so you can go about your days, the endeavor is doomed to fail. But then, this whole month has been a wild and fast lesson about finding balance: it is not a controlled homeostasis, but rather patience with oneself as the body and mind constantly adapt to the changing conditions of life. The fulcrum of the balance is a positive vision of oneself, a goal so to speak, but not too far ahead in the future.

After a month without a prolonged, hot shower in abundant soap, my skin is taking on a salty, ripe scent. It actually makes me want to get closer to people, not keep away from them, because it's something about me that I can share with them, somehow. I imagine that they want to be closer to me. I want to be closer to me.

Part of my contentment today is having enough of what I really like to eat, and not just enough, but almost too much. Up in the hills I want meat, beans and salt, but down at sea level I want fruit and biscuits. It's quite a simple equation but it took me some time to understand it. It could be psychological, that my isolation up here puts the focus on nutrition in case I can't get down to the store again. That's part of the reason I hate when I'm stuck with just rice and olive oil.

A glorious day it's been, adapting to the most recent changes, sunning in the window, and taking in the simple, charming goodness of the people around me.

Sicily 6/28/24

The view from the big window of my *rifugio* has a foreground of hazelnut forest, a middle-ground of two mountain ridges with a clay-roofed village on top of each, while the smooth waters of the Tyhrrenian Sea form the background, with a northern horizon. I cannot see the sun itself rise or set, but I watch the sky fill and then drain of color at the beginning and end of each day.

It took half of June for me to even care, and I'm aware of how jaded that sounds. But it was as if I had forgotten how to take in beauty at all, or particularly when it forms the backdrop of everyday life. When your eyes are taking in strip malls, slovenliness, total disregard for nature and public good, you cease questioning whether this is the stage on which your life is to play out, and you cease to question how this affects what you think about your life.

Walking through the glowing forest at dusk last night, the cloudless sky over the sea shades of pink and orange, for the first time it moved me, or rather, for the first time I was able to be moved by it. In that my heart was lifted up as it used to be in childhood.

I was not able to overcome the distance to the sea on my own two feet. It has a cost. Either it has the social cost of relying on others, or it has the monetary cost of having to call a taxi. The limitations imposed upon me have clarified how deeply I do value the shore, closer to the horizon. But it has also made me appreciate my life up here in the hills, looking out at it. The cool air, the kind villagers, the windowsill where I can read in the afternoon sun, the abundant work to be done. Prior to yesterday, I was trapped in a kind of battle with the constant availability of the sea (by right or by might, by bus or by foot), and I was always asking myself what I wanted, rather than feeling alive in what I had, or making efforts towards what I didn't have. Today will be just like yesterday, at home.

When the Sicilians find out that I'm not married, they say, *But where is your man? How are you doing without a man? Is he coming here? Do you have a man here in Sicily?*, even, *Are you able to sleep at night?* Sometimes I just put my hands over the left half of my chest and mime the heart breaking.

My vocabulary doesn't extend very far, certainly not far enough to describe my sleeplessness in New York, along with the rashes, an ebbing-and-flowing death wish, the chain smoking, and paralysis of soul, none of which are present after a month here. As my life comes more and more into balance on this island, the more fondly I think of him, the more I expect to find him waiting for me, to run and jump into his arms after being apart, as I did last summer when we first met.

But the thing about love and individual needs is that there has to be some agreement between them. Especially when an individual need is manifesting as a strongly-held, dearly-kept vision, from that otherworldly part of the soul. Otherwise, it will all come to tears.

Usually the cicadas start singing around my birthday in early August, but here they are a month earlier. It's my absolute favorite sound in the summer, besides that of a thunderstorm rolling in. The Greeks said that the cicadas are the voice of a handsome prince, beloved by the goddess of the dawn, who was granted eternal life but not eternal youth. Only his voice remains as his body has shriveled.

Sicily 6/29/24

My home is a former winery with a bulbous, 200 liter glass decanter sitting in the corner. I don't know that anyone would have lived and died in it. Although, I also don't know how old the building is and the uses it may have gone through. The house is quiet, nothing creaks or groans, I only hear sounds of life: insects flying in and out, the family across the street with two teenagers, birds singing and plucking elderberries, the mouse that lives under the roof tiles, distant sheep and roosters, the church bells, and sometimes a car.

The upper floor has been stuccoed, the floor is concrete as well as the sleeping platform, which has a small chamber embedded in it for the bucket that holds the water for the gravity shower downstairs. I leave the big window open at night for the cool forest air, which invites in mosquitoes and occasionally a dragonfly, certainly lots of moths, but it doesn't bother me anymore.

As for an afterlife, I do believe that the soul carries on.

The last week or so, the mosquitoes have been fewer but I've been getting that sensation of not being alone. That sensation in itself is often a self-fulfilling prophecy, it only needs to be thought once and then it will keep coming back, so I try not to give it too much credence.

I awake shortly after falling asleep but well after midnight, none too pleased about it, and disturbed by the dream I was having. I try to close my eyes, but keep opening them. The room doesn't get completely dark because of the warm, orange glow of the village streetlights, and my eyes scan the room. Of course, it is just an empty room.

I turn over onto my stomach and prop myself on my elbows. *If there's a spirit here, you have to leave and go back to the light,* I say. At least, it gives me a sense of control over my fear of the dark, like a low wall to climb on to get away from a dog.

A moment later there's an enormous, dull *thump* directly next to me, like someone has stomped their foot on the concrete floor with all their might.

Of course, it startles me. The thump occurs in the absence of anything physically moving.

Needless to say, I slept with the lights on after that.

And yet, a little poltergeist is just the other side of the coin, isn't it? For the forest at dusk to be filled with sprites and nearly phosphorescent as the last rays of sun meld with the coming night, our world has to be layered with worlds we can't see, but can sense in the liminalities of time and consciousness.

Liminal, the space between. Limit, the end of the space. Missed opportunity in not wanting to touch either.

My seamstress's brain, which has to be able to visualize not only the end, but each step in the right order in all three dimensions, often turned inside out, sees life at this moment being cut and assembled from a flat piece. The cloth, you could say, would be the questions in need of an answer: the flatness of the idea. And then I go into that great void of space and begin to cut and stitch something together to give it form.

How bad is it really, to have a poltergeist? Wouldn't the muse be the same kind of figure? Does that mean I'm also afraid of the muse? I'll only know by being alone in a room with them: the liminal.

If my body and soul cannot adapt to a way of life, sapping my will with prolonged, mysterious illnesses and mental turbidity, how will I ever know whether those missing elements of life, which I long for, are not actually necessary, unless I go and seek them? Should I not seek them with my whole being, should I take no risks, there would be no hope of ever knowing the limit.

I think these are the only two places, so to speak, that truly interest me. Though I seem to be someone who revels in routine, domesticity, and contemplation, they are all in the service of what I cannot see, and what I do not yet know.

Sicily 7/1/24

It's so hot and sticky in Sicily today that clothing feels like punishment. Cold water offers a brief rebirth before one is cast back into the stinking world of the body.

Bella, bella Sicilia. I've begun to mourn leaving Sicily already. But I do have a tale to tell of today. Let's see if I can tell it well, as the afternoon wanes, and the sleepless night begins to creep up on me.

God's ways are mysterious, aren't they? I would have tortured myself all summer walking up and down the mountain, if the road weren't blocked by those dogs in the lower village. Blocked by my worst fear, rational or not.

But where there is Scylla, there is Charybdis (Not far from here at all, in the Straight of Messina). To avoid the devouring monster, one risks getting sucked into the whirlpool. The whirlpool in this case being the loss of my independence, perhaps having to turn tail and fly back to America, if I can't figure out a way to get home from town on my own. Catching a ride with Giro and his family in the morning is never a problem, but they only stay at the beach for an hour because of the baby, so I say goodbye when we park and disappear.

I was so consumed by the fear that I would fail to secure a vehicle and have to pass the dogs, and that I would ultimately have to leave Sicily, that I couldn't sleep. Giro came knocking at 8:00 a.m., as promised.

In town, I took pleasure in neither figs, nor grapes, nor sun, nor water. I planned to take the 11:22 train to the next town, the cape with its hotels and beach clubs and tourists. Not to enjoy myself, but in the hopes of being able to get a taxi, just to prove that I could.

When I arrived, a mere eight minute journey, there were no taxis at the train station. Over and over again, I refreshed the taxi apps, to no avail. Given what was at stake, I had no qualms about entering into the mysterious, masculine realm of the station *tabaccheria* to buy a pack of Lucky Strikes. What could I do but pick up a few groceries, and walk around in the heat while my bowels churned, while I bled through my underwear and sweat like a pig, smoking to calm my nerves?

Giro texted, asking if I was enjoying the beach.

Ultimately, I ended up in a pew below the Jesus mosaic. All the shops were closing for the afternoon. Utterly defeated, I went to the ocean to rinse off. The pebbly shoreline tends to form a ridge, unlike the sandy, tapered shores of the Atlantic. A few steps out and you can let yourself fall in, to float in the warm, velvet water. In the sea, all is right with the world.

My phone was almost dead.

I recalled a younger, more intrepid version of myself, arriving one morning in Jutland with a flip phone, pretending to be a hotel guest to gain access to a lobby computer to find a couch to sleep on that night.

I'm a little old to be pretending, so when I walked into the hotel, I told the truth. A quarter of an hour later, a taxi driver walked in, nodded at me and said, *Her?*, and off we went.

The drive along the coast from the cape back to my town was spectacularly beautiful, as the sun cuts through the ocean to its depths, dredging up all the shades of blue. I sat in the front seat, and by the end of the drive we were on good terms and quite jocular. He told me to call him directly whenever I need a ride from town, and he'll give me a discount since there's no middle man.

Like the first time I made it up the mountain on foot, I walked to my door with an irrepressible smile on my face. I can stay, and set my mourning aside for a little while longer.

Sicily 7/2/24

Forty-eight hours of wakefulness brings on a sleep of great significance.

Thunderstorms have blown in from the south, one of which woke me at midnight from a dream about *il mio ragazzo*, with a broken leg, losing grip of my hand and slipping down a black, churning waterfall.

On a rare day of wind and cold, my *rifugio* lives up to its name, encapsulating the warm, pleasant sensation of being alive within it. I have melba toast, coffee, and the rest of the Lucky Strikes, for better or for worse.

Today is for reading, writing, and the washboard (sweat needs to be washed out right away).

Perhaps it is the lingering smell of tobacco, or that I sit a mere 180 miles from where he was born, or perhaps it was the spirit that stomped on the floor at night, but the feeling of having come home to this place is not my feeling at all, it is rather my grandfather's loss, in the year 1938, being un-lost. After all, the poltergeist woke me and made itself known a little after midnight on the twentieth anniversary of his death.

You can't send me away, the spirit was saying, *don't you recognize me?*

In the first months of the pandemic, I was awake in the early hours of the morning, having nowhere to be, and for a moment my room filled with daylight. That's the only way I can describe it, not as a flash or burst, but that it was night, then it was day, and then it was night again. In the morning I learned that my great uncle, my grandfather's brother, had passed away during the night.

To pursue the individual life takes a great deal of trust, not only in oneself, but in the well-ordered hierarchy that starts with God, below Him the angels, the saints, then those we love who have passed, then those we love who remain on earth, and only at the very bottom does trust in oneself come into play.

Had I not been saved so many times on my foolish adventures, I might not know this.

Sicily 7/5/24

I'm not one to pour my heart out publicly, though having this travel diary is teaching me to prune my thoughts for an audience. For five years, I recorded every day of my life in private, often in great detail, until I decided to try writing for others. Sicily is less personal, it's an adventure of sorts, which I don't mind sharing.

It was cold and cloudy, and then rained for two days. Nobody went outside, the hills were quiet, and I even had to light the stove for warmth. Unfortunately, I ran through all of my wood, and the wood in the forest is wet. How am I going to cook today?

But I was out of food, so I decided to walk to the next village to the butcher shop. I've been wanting to go there, but was afraid that it would be less welcoming than the shop in town, less understanding of a foreigner coming around, although I have yet to meet an unfriendly Sicilian. Coming around the first turn out of the village, I was greeted by a man up on his porch, high above the road. I often see him there, and the other day he was listening while Giro's sister-in-law yelled down to me from her balcony several floors up, introducing herself, asking me about myself. He asked if I was going to town, but I said, No, just to the village to go to the butcher.

I continued on my way, a little edgy because I'm always afraid a beast is going to jump out of nowhere now. Ten minutes down the road, the neighbor I had just spoken to pulled over. He had come down to give me a lift. We went to the *snack* where they have some dried goods and a bar, and then to the butcher. When he got out of the car, I noticed that he had a very badly curved spine and walked hunched over. This must be why he is often out on his porch, sitting. His name is Francesco.

The butcher grew up in Australia, of all places, so I was able to order in English, a steak and two lamb chops. She pulled a fresh lamb carcass out of the fridge, hung it up, hacked off a leg, and cut off the chops for me. If I ever need to go to town, she said, just come to the butcher shop and she'll find me a lift the rest of the way, she knows everyone. I imagine the lamb comes from the farm down the road from the spring, where I often hear sheep bleating.

Back at home, I was sitting in my windowsill when there was a car horn and a whistle downstairs, my old friend Giro, saying hello. Yes, the island is coming back to life after the rain. The sky is hazy today, but last night I saw every star in the sky. I sat in the window looking up at them as the odor of smoldering cherry wood billowed from the stovepipe above my head.

On my table with the bright yellow tablecloth, a Sicilian folk pattern, sits an unfinished letter, the latest draft of the nine or so I burned, and my heart sank when I walked in from the shopping trip and remembered that I had been up all night, writing, tearing off the sheets and crumbling them into the stove, over and over. But I didn't weep until long after the sun was up, when I went back and read the last paragraph I had written to him, the one who is far away.

I'm a little disturbed by my own defense mechanisms, that I can be so engrossed in my surroundings that I won't shed a tear for two or three weeks, and then out of nowhere, his voice, and his eyes, and the grasp of his hand while we sat weeping on a fire escape the night before I left, that neither of us could pinpoint why being together was impossible when neither of us wanted to leave the other, blots out everything around me. Where am I? How did I get here? When we first separated in May and I returned home, I woke up every night in the dark, confused, flailing my arms, grasping for him, not knowing where I was. It's a similar feeling, except in the daylight.

But something has shifted and is moving into its rightful place, because the music has started to come to me too. All of the reasons that I am here, to embrace chaos, to not know what tomorrow will bring, to be in the land that my spirit longs for, to understand the place of this great love in my life, to live a life that is worth writing about, to see if the muse can be summoned by enough silence, to collect wood and water, to eat lamb, and to mourn what I may never have returned to me, all of these reasons are quite real and I must bow down to them, I must be guided by them.

I am lucky, I know that. I have nothing, and yet I have everything I could wish for. Perhaps someday, everything I have will be under the same roof.

The church bells chime noon.

Sicily 7/6/24

Six hours on the beach today. An ocean like bathwater. Skin almost dark enough to not burn at all. Food shopping in the early evening. Taxi home.

I thought I had saved the number for the taxi driver, but it turned out that I hadn't. Giovanni…Giovanni…looking through my contacts, he wasn't there. I could have kicked myself. He promised to give me a discount.

But I had asked the girl at the hotel the other day for the taxi company's number, just in case. I called and ordered a cab. Twenty minutes later, the driver picked up me up at the train station. I don't know what it is, but there's something so refined about ordering a car. You set your groceries down and somebody puts them in the car for you. Happily, I pay for the the privilege. Especially when I'm tired, sun-soaked, and carrying pounds and pounds of groceries.

I was in the blue, blue ocean this afternoon and burst into tears, though no one noticed. How could anyone notice tears in the ocean? When I went back to my towel to lay down, I kept crying, and blew my nose into it. I recorded eight minutes of my thoughts about my lost love and sent them to him, which relieved me.

When I got out of the taxi tonight in front of Giro's open garage, he said, *Che deve fare un ragazzo qua?*, What's a boy to do here? I think he thought the taxi driver was some young man I convinced to give me a ride up the mountain. *Niente*, I said, rolling my eyes. *Nothing.*

It's the same answer I give whenever he comes by the door and asks what I'm doing, *Che fai? Niente.*

Sicily 7/9/24

This really *is* the best life, where your actions and the outcome of your actions all occur within view, no middle man, just a roof over your head and the motivation of necessity, an end in itself. What is made by hand is more beautiful, and a life lived by hand, so to speak, is more beautiful.

I accept that most of my time is spent up here in the hills, looking out at the ocean but not able to swim in it, thinking about people but only able to imagine them down in the city. Up here, far from vice.

But I've been very lenient with myself about spiritual and intellectual labors left undone. These labors are in opposition to vice, but living far from vice does not make good labor effortless. Vice is effortless, with its hypnotic pull, whereas the labors of the soul, or you could say any labor of virtue, requires voluntary suffering and offers little to no reprieve from suffering.

I suppose that makes three: necessary action, virtue, and vice. Which is a distillation of what brought me to Sicily.

Necessity is a good medicine, I am finding, for all parts of myself. But what is not taken up by necessity hangs in the balance between vice and virtue, because there is always sloth, the sin of omission, the sin against one's responsibilities. And what are my responsibilities here? What are my responsibilities towards life?

Do we turn to vices at any time other than when we are feeling weak and afraid, or apathetic? They fill the emptiness that should be filled with courage in facing the unknown.

There have been so many unknowns in Sicily, and the rug has been pulled out from under me so many times, that finally, the hard lesson has been won: the difference between panic and calm is not control, but trust in a good outcome without it.

I consider it a matter of faith, naturally. Needing divine intervention nourishes the bond with the divine and safeguards the divine will against human complaint. And conversely, if you never ask for help, you never receive any; if you think you're in control, you'll never notice a *deus ex machina*.

Yesterday, early in the evening, I gave up trying to do anything and laid down in bed. I just listened to people, chattering on an evening walk, or out sweeping the front of the house, talking to a neighbor, or the family across the way arguing, as usual. Giro gave my door a good knock but I pretended not to be home, and this morning I told him I'd had a headache, which wasn't true. It took hours and hours to fall asleep, and I read only a few pages of *Leaves of Grass* until it got too dark to see.

That is, I chose neither vice nor virtue. I had no fear, and I needed no courage to lay in my bed, half drifting to sleep, half drifting in thought, nor could you call it necessary. That's the state of my soul at the moment, and tonight, I think I'll do the same.

My time here will be half over in a week, and I will be content if I can say that with the first half, I learned to lay quietly at dusk, in order to find some endeavor of virtue for which I needed, and asked for, divine intervention, and that I was afraid, but chose courage over vice.

Sicily 7/13/24

The blue jay was squawking, caught in the blackberry brambles at the side of the road. Luckily, I was out for my evening walk, so I picked up a stick and gently freed him. I thought, maybe that was the crux of my existence; in some grand scheme of energy and karma and interconnectedness, the only thing I absolutely had to do was free that blue jay, and none of the rest of it matters.

I've been up in the village, mostly at home, waking regularly at dawn and slowly chipping away at my pantry staples of beans, rice and lentils. Meat, apples and zucchini ran out days ago, but I haven't wanted for anything. After all, I'm trying to give myself a chance to put down my burdens and return to a state that is closer to what God intended for a human being.

It's been a convalescent week of sorts, which was due. June was a month of preparation, where I weaned myself off of habitual excess, both physical and mental, and ironed out all the practicalities of living here in the *rifugio*. I was unconsciously preparing for the dam to break in July, as reminders of the troubles I am so keen to solve would resurface, as they always do.

I've been talking about this since May: if there is a poisoned or disrupted quality to all natural goods in America, what happens to you if you go somewhere where the natural goods are still good?

The hills here are dotted with human habitation, everywhere you turn you are embraced by the image of man having triumphed ever so slightly over nature, just enough to flourish, while still living in accord with the original creation. Whereas driving through a similar landscape in the American West, a hilly brushland, offers nothing but emptiness, a feral loneliness, man alongside the land, either ignoring it or using it.

I knew that my state of being was going to clash with *what it might have been* if it had only known Sicily, never America. With a change of air to a place that is naturally endowed with all the elements of human well-being, the healing element is not only in the leaving behind, but also in the adjusting to what is good. The result has been a week of suffering, and I speak of suffering generally: there is no physical suffering that is not also of the heart and mind, and vice versa.

In *Kolyma Stories,* Varlam Shalamov remarks on how quickly the horses die compared to the men, although they are all in the notorious Siberian gulag, the goldmine at Kolyma. Human understanding allows for greater adaptability, an inability to give up, in the face of suffering.

The bird in the bramble or the horse in the mine will die if they cannot free themselves, but not you or I. Man is more creative, perhaps too creative, and he will simply uproot the bramble and carry it with him to a new place, hoping that it will not take root where he sets it down. He will still stoke a fire and cook himself dinner, and ponder what he was doing when he got into that bramble, and how he might yet get out of it. He may curse himself, he may pray to God, he may entangle himself further, he may give up for days, weeks, years at a time. But he'll die of something else first.

And he will never know if his freedom was more meaningful than a blue jay's.

Sicily 7/16/24

Va bene, va bene. Despite my extraordinary laziness, my talent with foreign languages is starting to shine through. I no longer stare blankly when people speak to me, I can often understand the gist of what they're saying. The downside of this is that if I understand enough, but someone is not addressing me, I assume they're talking about me, thinking that I understand *niente*. (I might be right, after all.)

I was not surprised that my taxi driver tonight knew Giro. Everyone knows Giro and Giro knows everyone. At the spring the other day, a village acquaintance of mine told me Giro is "coo-coo", but what does it matter? What is the definition of "coo-coo" here?

The driver and I were chatting about the village on the drive up the mountain. He knows the village well because his grandmother lived nearby, although she passed away two years ago and he hasn't been back since. *And then there's Giro, the bricklayer, who lives on the corner.* - Yes, I caught a ride to town with him this morning, everyone is very nice. - *That's because they're all Jehovah's Witnesses!* I burst out laughing. What? Isn't everyone Catholic here? Anyway, Giro doesn't go to church on Sundays, he stops at my door and whistles to get my attention.

When we pull up, Giro is in his garage as usual and we clarify that he is not, in fact, a Jehovah's Witness.

Earlier today I had the beach to myself, because I was there at the most brutal time of day, between noon and 4:00 p.m. It's only possible to lay on the beach for a half hour until you have to cool off in the ocean again. There's no transition between air and water, it's just a few steps across the burning hot sand, an awkward fumbling over the large rocks where the waves break, and then you are floating in a salty bath.

I had the biggest bunch of grapes I've ever seen in my life, and I took them with me into the water. I waded in up to my waist, plucking grape after grape in the Mediterranean, shoving them into my mouth under the shade of my cotton hat. When the grapes were done, I went in up to my chest and took a stroll parallel to the shore, back and forth, in the crystal water. I could see my feet at the bottom, and the little sun fish swimming around them, which were not interested in my grape offerings.

At a certain point, between the heat, the lulling music of the waves, the cloudless sky, the solitude, the hazy air, I felt out of body. My mind was running, but I wasn't really there. My stomach was churning from too many grapes, but I didn't care.

I left in the late afternoon to go shopping, sucked back into the modern world with all of its choices, its vices, and the inexplicable dance music of the supermarket. I'm tempted to buy everything I want, not what I need, because I know I'll be calling a taxi home. Melba toast is a great extravagance. Nevertheless, I buy a multitude of legumes, oats, and paper towels. I train my mind on the freedom I felt all week up in the hills, subsisting on nothing but pulses, salt and water, and how absolutely fine I felt. Just me, my suffering, and my subsistence.

At the butcher shop, I combine my knowledge of "one kilo" and "a half kilo" to order one and a half kilos of beef. I've gone a full week without meat, and while it hasn't been terrible, considering that I'm not exercising all that much and have no wood at the ready for cooking, I want those extra 500 grams.

I drag my tired limbs into the hazelnuts to collect deadwood off the forest floor so I can cook. I cook and eat my fill and there's plenty left for breakfast.

What else is there to say? That was my day in Sicily.

Sicily 7/17/24

I was down at the lower terrace of the hazelnut grove looking up into the canopy to find branches without leaves. Those are the dead shoots, which I can pull down to the ground and bring home for firewood. The grove was pleasant, vibrating with the sound of cicadas, and my mind was free to wander.

All morning I had been drawing sketches of the summer house I would build if I could. A summer house without insulation or running water, a place to be closer to Life. Even if I find myself in the arms of my lost love again in September, it won't make me loathe New York any less. Even if somebody handed me all the trappings of success overnight, it wouldn't make modern life any less of a cage. The way I want to live is the way I am living now.

Sicily is hardly my first venture into an unknown world, but it is the first one to make me understand that I have to defend the fact of my thinking differently, of dreaming differently, and defend it with my life. Figuratively speaking, for no one has a gun to my head, but I can be punished, ostracized, otherwise forced into an emotional or physical exile, which is a form of death for a social animal.

I either sacrifice the potential to live a life that springs from *what I know to be good*, or I let it be sacrificed to what others find good (but which I know not to be good at all).

Enough of my life has been wasted that way. It has been the scaffolding of these many years that seemed inordinately painful for someone still young.

And so, I was standing there in the shade of the hazelnut trees when the voice of Sicily whispered to me, saying, Even if those who could help you want you to be quiet and meek, to leave them in peace, don't leave them in peace; their sleep is not the sleep of a clean conscious, it is the sleep of one who has forgotten how to dream.

Who built this old house in Sicily but someone who dreamt of it first, and fit together stone after stone, and shoved even smaller stones in between the big ones, and cut down trees and stood them on end in between the stones, and cut down more trees and laid them across the top to support the roof? Who planted the vineyard for the wine that was made in this room?

Our time on earth for many millennia was all dreaming. Man had first to conceive of the individual developments that led to the heights of human civilization, that led to the creation of a paradise like Sicily. Sicily would not be paradise if it were barren of human touch. Perhaps for cacti and geckos, but even they love to grow and sun themselves on the stones that have been stacked into walls.

Sicily whispers this to you constantly, even when you are just looking out at the sea and hear nothing, saying, Trust only the wisdom of those who have known me.

Sicily 7/20/24

The grapes growing wild along the road are turning purple and losing their tartness. The blackberry brambles are putting forth fruit to make up for all of the times they've drawn blood.

The dog days of summer are here, and I'm up in the hills like everyone else. Yesterday, I couldn't stop sleeping. I had breakfast and slept until lunch, I had lunch and slept again until dinner, I had dinner and wrote in the windowsill in the evening, and then fell into a deep sleep again until morning. But as I was falling asleep at night, I was too conscious of it, and became afraid, and kept waking myself up. I don't know how many times that happened before I relented.

I finally received the offer I've been waiting for all summer, which was for Giro to lend me his electric saw. Earlier today, he heard me breaking branches deep in the hazelnut grove, and descended down the terraced hillside to tell me to follow him over to his property at the end of the street.

The stone walls of the ancient houses are more durable than the wood and tile rooftops. Like the house next door to me, which has become a walled garden where the elderberry grows, the structures return partly to nature. Giro's chicken coop is built out of one of these old homes. He has another enclosure for turtles, a few rows of zucchini and beans, and some young fruit trees, in addition to his plot at the other end of the village with olives, lemons and oranges.

We dragged deadwood out of the forest, he cut it down to pieces, and I loaded up my wagon and walked it down to my house. Finally, my firewood rack is full. I gathered all of the gnarled and oddly shaped pieces and a bucket of kindling, brought them upstairs, and lit the stove. I've found that heating up my room when it's already the hottest part of the day makes no difference.

Hot is hot. First, I cooked rice for lunch, then I boiled water for laundry, and finally I set the pot of fava and Scicli beans on the stove, which had been soaking since yesterday.

And then, with the last of my energy, I walked to both springs, once for drinking water and once for bathing water. I don't like taking the wagon anymore because everybody has an opinion about it. I'd rather just take the jug in my backpack twice.

Lately, every time I reach for my phone, I've been asking myself what I am trying to avoid thinking about. This reminds me that there is important activity going on in the background of my mind that I shouldn't drown out.

Mainly, this synthesis is causing my to look back at my life and feel that it was all an illusion. This isn't to say that earthly life isn't real. The events happened, the emotions were real, the outcomes and consequences were real, time passed. Rather, people build their lives and sense of self on all kinds of delusions, and then we subject ourselves to them, or are subjected to them, as if they were true. In effect, we are all poisoned by human delusion, sometimes in a trickle and sometimes in a burst.

But I feel light and free when I think of this. I've blamed myself for a lot, punished myself for a lot, and it was all delusion, all illusion. Maybe another day I'll say more, but not tonight. I'm much too tired and have some mosquitoes to kill before I can sleep.

Sicily 7/21/24

The matter is settled now: it's the fault of the New World.

The New World is lacking too much that is central to human happiness and well-being. The other day, I was describing to you how a stone house in Sicily will lose its roof, given enough time, and as the forest encroaches upon the house, the house becomes a part of the forest again. The forest has only been changed in that man took the stones out of the ground and stacked them on top of each other. Man improves upon the forest in this way. No one can deny that an ancient ruin set into the trees is a thing of beauty.

Human culture is nothing more than a well-developed habitat, which encompasses all of man's faculties, from his ability to build himself a dwelling, to the songs he sings while he works, to the food he produces to keep himself alive. Man is a part of the land. Each generation only refines and increasingly canonizes the elements of the area, a form of natural selection.

Take that man out of his habitat and he will suffer, just like any other animal. What is the New World but a menagerie of human beings taken out of their natural habitat?

You see, a person cut loose from everything that is supposed to protect them, as an en-souled being, as one who loves and is loved, is much more vulnerable. He will have no choice but to partake in whatever will help him to meet his needs, and there will be no inheritance to give him a leg up in life. Perhaps a few generations down the line, but that inheritance will come with heavy losses, the loss of everything that was supposed to guide his descendants, through every one of their days from birth to death.

I came to this conclusion sitting in my windowsill, as I do every evening, looking at the castle on the far ridge. But the intuition of this being the eventual conclusion has dogged me longer than I can remember, and with a particular vengeance over the last half year.

Massive migration in the industrial age: a world was built that no one would have chosen to build otherwise. It was not built at a human scale. What are we supposed to do with it? What is it supposed to do with us?

I came into this world, like all other infants, perfect, innocent. Oh, poor babe of the New World, your life will be spent in search of something that was taken from you, long before you were ever born.

Sicily 7/25/24

The weather the other night was reminiscent of early autumn in Pennsylvania. Soft rain, soft wind, a chill in the air, and all of the birds and insects had fallen quiet. The precipitation let up at dusk, so I set out into the misty, darkening world to get water for the morning. Wearing long pants and a cotton sweater, I stood at the spring waiting for the 15 liter jug to fill up, my third trip to the spring, the first being at dawn after staying up all night, and the second after sleeping for an hour. A pine marten paused at the edge of the hazelnut grove, then darted across the street to the forest.

The martens have been all over the past week, although this is the first I'm seeing of them. On my walk through the damp woods yesterday morning, trying to catch the last scent of the rain, I followed a marten that was trotting down the road ahead of me. It froze when a car passed at the top of the ridge, as the roosters were playing a game of call-and-answer across the valley. Although I wouldn't get too close, they have sweet dispositions. They remind me of the orange cat in the village that I've named Piccola, and her three kittens, the way that they pause and stare, and scamper away from you. I once ran into Piccola in the forest when I wandered off the road, she must have been hunting geckos.

I picked up a translation job, a play from the Weimar Republic, and it will help me to exist with absolute impunity for a little bit longer. It cancels out my rent for the entire summer, which wasn't difficult to do. Sitting here, toggling between the play and this diary, my favorite neighbor stopped by the door and called up to me. I came down and she dropped a huge handful of plums into my hands, the tiny purple ones that taste like jam when they're overripe.

Where was I?

The irony of having had a few too many obstacles to a straightforward life, is that you find yourself free in a way you never would have had the courage for, had someone laid out the options before you. Maybe you believe that your soul chose an incarnation, or like me, you have a relationship to a higher intelligence and believe in His good will towards you (which oftentimes comes across as senseless torture), maybe you have been captured by existential nihilism: but may you be granted a life where your back is against the wall most of the time, because that's where you have to start thinking.

When the rain makes me think of home, the place that I couldn't get far enough away from at the start of June, it doesn't start my stomach churning as much at the end of July. The loss of love, of control, of my way, all of that has mellowed, and none of it is as it seemed.

Love left me a long message on the night of the rain (the summer is short, after all), Ambition has stood up and can now see above the dense wood of limited inspiration (to the horizon, where ocean and sky become indistinguishable).

Over thousands of words, over the many weeks here, I've been trying to put together some sense of what life means in one context or another, what it means to exist as physical animals, what it means over the course of a lifetime, over the course of lives that spill into each other over the generations, what it means in the course of a summer in solitude.

An acquaintance sent me pictures of the *Gründerzeitbau* in Zagreb, an echo of Austro-Hungary, under the warm glow of yellow streetlights. My father's people also once lived in the Empire, but they left for America, and like so many other Slovaks, worked at the Steel. I accompanied my father to Slovakia a decade ago during a sunny, perfect October. Everywhere we went, he wanted to go to the graveyards to look for our family name, but we never found it. He remembers his *Zedo*'s body laid out in the living room of a row-house, with a big gray mustache, sometime in the mid 1950's.

People don't just start over when they cross the ocean. No one really understands what it does to a person, nor does anyone understand the forces at play in the lives that come into being on the other side. These unknowns have such a hold on me because the weight on my shoulders has always seemed too heavy to only be my own.

That said, the revelation forcing its way to the surface over many years and finally seeing the light in Sicily, is that the time has come to forgive. I think anyone, in looking back at their life, would weep bitterly (as I did) if they concluded that the time had come to forgive. Who wants to forgive? If it were easy, we wouldn't mull over slights for decades, we wouldn't ruin ourselves instead of moving on, if it were easy.

When I decided to give up my degenerate big-city life, I truly believed that I had failed to uphold the standards of normalcy. That I had failed to grab the baton, so to speak, because I had to give up drinking, which is something that normal people shouldn't have to do. But I've had a change of heart and now see that there's nothing normal about a normalcy that looks at epidemic despair, addiction crises, rampant non-infectious disease—clear signs on their own that something has gone wrong—and points the finger at man himself. No, man needs to point his finger back at that world. My finger is trained towards home, northeastward past the islands.

And yet, Sicily's purity will do me no good if I am nursing grievances.

For the first and only time, the nebulous concept of the mind/body connection has been made comprehensible to me. There's a worldly explanation for my heated diatribes against the place—the physical place, but also its values—that I call the New World.

Every step that man takes away from his natural environment is a form of stress, every loss he grieves forever, every entrenched form of mistreatment handed down through a family, every job he endures for inadequate remuneration, every sin he holds against himself and doubly so the sins he holds against others, and then every drink and every cigarette to balance it out: his body wasn't built for this kind of normal.

And if he is an American on the Eastern Seaboard today, his environment is woefully filthy, and his diet disastrously short of what his body needs to maintain some semblance of cleanliness and equilibrium so that it does not become too diseased, in light of all this abnormality.

I thought I'd overcome anger because, outwardly, almost nothing riles me anymore. Then I set foot in Sicily with my body failing, a failed relationship, the failure to accrue any outward success, and found that I was actually quite angry towards the place I had just left behind. But I see how I am contributing to my own destruction by letting an undercurrent of resentment towards a broken world drip its venom into my body, day in and day out, and night after night in my dreams.

That's where forgiveness comes in. Only forgiveness towards a world I could not help being born into, towards a world I cannot change, can dry up that well of venom.

Humanity has known this for a long time, though, that the grounding principles of a good life on earth are fiber and clemency (Give us this day our daily bread, and forgive us our trespasses, as we forgive those who trespass against us). I had to visit paradise to be reminded, I suppose.

Sicily 7/26/24

It's early morning, I'm sitting in my windowsill watching the sky color in. There's been a strip of cumulus clouds sitting at the same place over the horizon, running east to west as far as I can see. I wonder if it's dust from Mt. Etna, and that's why they're heavy and unmoving, unlike regular clouds.

The light of someone's sailboat is glowing out in the ocean. Imagine how peaceful it must be out there, where there aren't any roosters. Oftentimes the haze over the sea blends the water and the air, forming one continuous blue from the shore all the way up to the heavens. Everything is so still, there is nothing to disrupt the fine water droplets hanging in the sky.

I'm awake early because I'm getting a ride to town just after 7:00 a.m. I can't wait to walk around after sitting and working on the translation for several days in a row.

Evening.

The last thing I wanted to do was scrounge the floor of the hazelnut grove for kindling, or pull down a dead sapling and drag it to my house, I didn't want to make the trip to the spring, but I was so hungry and I had to do all of it. I had bought that precious substance, red meat, and I was going to cook it.

There's an eerie quality to the island today. I noticed it in town this morning, rather, I was noticing the shabbiness, the disintegrating concrete, the empty cigarette cartons, the scrubby weeds in the park, and then as I came around the corner out of the forest tonight, the dust from Mt. Etna had eclipsed the sun, and it was nothing but a fiery red sphere hanging over the horizon. I stopped and stared at it a little too long. When I continued walking, I passed an old man with swollen ankles standing outside of his house, also staring at the sphere.

It was quarter after seven this morning when my neighbor across the street knocked and told me that Betta, Giro's wife, was waiting in her car for me. I grabbed my bags, locked my door and hurried to the intersection, not that I have to lock my door here. I'm never sure if Betta likes me, but we talked all the way and she invited me to a festival tomorrow night. The place they always drop me off is now unofficially known as *Frutta*, because I always buy fruit first thing and never have them drop me off at the beach. *Dove scendi? Frutta?*

I got a talking-to from a policeman who caught me illegally putting a whole trash bag into a city trash can. I gingerly offered to take my trash back, and all he did was explain to me that it has to be sorted.

Then I went straight to the beach because nothing was open yet. In the course of the day, I went swimming at three different beaches. I spent the mid-afternoon in the next town over, not really for any reason or that I like it there, just because I like riding the train. My town is much better, in fact it's perfect, there aren't any tourists, the beaches are quiet and I don't have to worry about leaving my things while I swim.

I went to my secret beach first, though, where inevitably someone strikes up conversation with me. It's like I've been learning Italian in my sleep, I don't know how it's possible that I'm able to hold a conversation when I've put in so little effort. I read a few paragraphs of a short story by Cesare Pavese, and again, couldn't remember when I learned to read Italian, but apparently I'm not bad at it. I do think it is partly the purity of the language that makes it so easy to pick up.

By the time I was back in my town in the late afternoon, a strong wind had kicked up, muddying the usually crystalline ocean. It was great fun diving into the waves and swimming against the current.

But now, it is time to sleep.

Sicily 7/28/24

I've alluded to the idea recently of entering into life uncorrupted.

I think I am coming around to Goethe's conclusion that *Sicily is the clue to everything*, in an existential sense. Man, woman, water, stone, air, trees, animals, dusk, dawn; I cannot look out over the mountains without seeing a fairly ideal outcome of this agreement between the raw material from the Creator and its inhabitants.

In Catholic doctrine, the soul enters and leaves the earthly realm in a state of purity. Throughout life there are as many opportunities to make amends as there are opportunities to go wrong, even a little leeway with purgatory.

These are really just two expressions of the same principle: what is of divine origin is perfect, what is of human origin has a tendency to corrupt, but if the latter adheres to the laws of the former, good can come of it.

Few are comfortable anymore with the idea that achieving this good is the purpose of life, leaving us instead with a duty to adhere to the standards of secular society. Except that secular normalcy is simply based on consensus. The consensus can draw up a list of its own commandments, moral or amoral, which can change at any time, and it has reduced us to a set of desires to be manipulated, vectors of disease, customers, bootlickers: as much as possible, we are supposed to forget we ever had souls.

For if you remain aware of your first breath outside the womb, and you are able to imagine that one day you will breathe your last, then you will remember that you were once perfect and you will again become perfect, and in fact the soul remains perfect throughout, underneath its patina: you would not defile it by handing it over to the consensus of men.

It's taken me my whole life to understand this.

It was that winter in the Berner Oberland, a grisly five and a half years ago, that opened a schism between what I had known and what I could choose instead. The moon rose over my life and stayed there while I set about reconciling all of the irreconcilables between the two. But the time has come for the moon to set, for Helios to hitch up his chariot and carry the sun to its high noontime position. As if this summer had followed that winter directly.

It's about time. Here I am at the eleventh hour burying the hatchet that made me, for you only have up through the end of your 33rd year to belong to your circumstances; thereafter your life belongs to the world.

I fill my bottles at the spring and make my way back up the hill, when lo and behold, there's a dog on the path around the first corner. I freeze, but it's plain that he's very old and completely disinterested in me. I watch for a minute or two as he turns and saunters away, trying to figure out why he seems familiar. But of course, he's the old dog from the village who's normally asleep in a crumbling stone barn behind a gate, and every once in a while musters the energy to bark at me. I think Piccola the cat lives at that same house.

Still, I turn around and walk back to the spring, down the hill and onto the main road. I pass Francesco's house, and he is on his porch as usual. He asks me where my *carrello* is, my cart, which I'm normally pulling behind me full of water jugs, except that I've grown tired of the cart and having been taking a single jug in a backpack instead.

If I only talked to men here, I'd think that I understood no Italian at all. But Francesco's wife pulls up in her car, and joins him on their porch. Women, unfailingly, simplify their language and slow down their speech so that I can understand; it must have something to do with the maternal instinct. The men speak in idioms at top speed and then look at me like I have two heads while I stand there squinting in concentration, at a complete loss, whereas with women I can hold a conversation, they speak to me like a child and fill the rest in with dramatic hand gestures.

English is beautiful and international, she says, unlike Italian with its complicated Latin grammar.

Sicily 7/30/24

There was that unmistakable burn at the back of my throat as I tossed and turned, sweating in the still July night. It blossomed into fits of sneezing, puffy eyes, sore joints, fatigue, a slight fever, and a sense of not really being where I am, just when I thought I was out of the woods after a rough month. Not that I have anywhere to be, but the ache in my hips makes my usual work position—leaning back in a chair with my legs up on the table—uncomfortable, and I have multiple pages of phonetically written, working class Berlin dialect to get through. This morning I was just barely able to drag myself down the path to the spring to fill a jug for washing, which I had to do because I have to shower twice a day.

Then there was the unmistakable sense that the *nonna* across the street had been looking at me funny recently. And then I overheard a heated conversation with her son, where my landlord was mentioned. I was biting my nails all day. What had I done? I'm quiet as a church mouse, I wouldn't talk to anyone if everyone wasn't always talking to me first. But it turned out that it's only my wood stove, the smoke is blowing into her house every day, and they worked it out. My landlord instructed me to go pick up a little gas burner in town later this week when it arrives in the mail.

I'm pleased with how well I've learned to take things in stride this summer. When I first arrived, every little change threw me into a fit, but yesterday I almost didn't care about the stove, almost didn't even worry what I was going to eat for the next week if I'm not supposed to burn wood. When I thought at certain points during those five hours, *Oh now I remember why we separated*, I laid my phone on my stomach and let him talk, and eventually we got onto pleasanter topics. The rule generally applies that whatever you fear has some truth to it), but for the most part it ends up being an annoyance, something that has to be worked around but which won't kill you.

These are the adventures of a feverish translator in the Sicilian highlands, and that's all she has for you tonight.

Sicily 8/1/24

August has come with its hint of autumn, as harvests ripen, leaves shrivel during the long days, the grass around the hazelnuts is cut and raked to dry in piles, the olives have taken on size and the towering wild fennel along the road has set its yellow flowers. July was weary, hardly anyone went out, but now we seem to have become collectively aware that it will all soon be over, as the night breezes cool.

I am not sure we give enough credit to each season, and its distinct set of three months. Especially when you arrive somewhere as a new-comer, with the intention of staying for that length of time, you have no choice but to let it wash over you at its will.

This third month is for preparing to leave, taking stock of what you have and have not yet done with your time. It is the most dangerous month psychologically, because of the pressure to see things through to their end, and this doesn't always happen under the control of the will. Towards the end of my time in the Alps, sometime in early February when I was starting to tie up loose ends, in some conversation about something, the farmer I worked for said to me, *In Träumen kann man alles*. In dreams you can do anything—spoken by a man who had chosen a beautiful but hard life, total self-sustainability, which prevented him from ever leaving his farm for more than a few hours in the afternoon, any day of his life. I think of it now because those words came along when my time there had reached that bridge between arriving and the question of what it would mean if I stayed past the season: whatever lay beyond that point belonged to dreams, and needed to remain in dreams. In life, you cannot do anything you want.

The freshness of my presence in this little village has begun to wane, and now that August is here I have to answer for it, such that the wood smoke eventually became intolerable to the neighbors. Or that, without naming any names, I was entreated upon for a *scopatini*, a little fuck, which was only the most direct of many such invitations. Two of my three water jugs have sprung a leak and I feel like my body is developing a permanent film by never having a hot shower. I don't know if I can tolerate the flies in the morning and the mosquitoes at night for much longer.

But early August is a mirage, you just have to be wiser than its tricks. By insisting that you only *scopare* with the *ragazzo* you still love and, no, you aren't lying, you become beatified into a *brava ragazza*, a good girl, and she's even more beloved.

Because you do not do just anything, for a mirage disintegrates into chaos and uncertainty with time, regardless. And see how I have forgotten that this day in late summer, in the chaos and uncertainty of the present, was also once a dream? Have you noticed that I have tried to jump ahead to hallucinations of what will become, what will be built on the foundation of this very season that, in actuality, I might spend the rest of in fantasy?

No, I can't let that happen. It is only in responding to those pressures that can no longer be contained, particular to those three months, that you become *brav*, good, and maybe even brave.

On another note, the ghost returned last night. The guitar sounded twice on its own, a few minutes apart. I thought perhaps a string had loosened and then snapped from a change in temperature, but this morning it was in perfect order and tune.

Sicily 8/2/24

The only state the human being really longs for is synthesis, a total blurring of the divide between self and other, self and world, self and action, to become what *is* so deeply as to be unable to reflect on it and thus be released from the pain of consciousness.

This is a noble and natural goal and is served in its positive form by love, prayer and meditation, bearing children, masterful work, and in its negative form by drugs, violence, and scrolling, to name a few. I think if only we were honest with ourselves about wanting to experience oneness, it would be less daunting and we wouldn't seek it out in its lesser forms. I've discussed already, probably more than anyone wants to hear, our separation from nature, our loss of synthesis with nature—which has snowballed into a loss of synthesis in all realms of life, so that we do not even know to expect it, nor do we know that we are missing it.

I enjoy the synthesis of the village, even if I have to hear the conversations inside the house across the street, and everyone is watching my every move. Well, I should say that people my age and younger are relatively ambivalent towards me. It's the older people who have reacted most strongly to my presence, and I think that has to do with their experience of integration into life itself. I've heard the older women talking about me right outside my own house, and in their defense, I don't understand much, but there's a kind of performative gossip and interest in my—truly, insignificant—comings and goings which is meant to guard against my presence. Naturally, the older men are constantly offering to help me, to drive me around, they ask me too many questions, and I learned that they, too, took my presence to be a kind of wild and unknowable element, something that dropped out of the sky and commanded full attention. But those young enough to have integrated into the infinite global social web, have a non-reaction to me. Overall, however, the strong social homogeneity and cohesion in Sicily, and the presence of traditional social life in public spaces, has reminded me that we are actually supposed to experience a synthesis with the people around us in the form of awareness, given and withheld.

While I have a large extended family which preserves some of this function, a family is much more forgiving than the instinct of preservation in a wider, interdependent social schema.

In the village, at least when you approach a friend, you pinch all your fingers together and shake your hand, tilt your head back as if to show off your chin, knit your brows and say *Che fai?!*, What are you doing?!, like an accusation. At first I thought it was a joke, maybe it is, but I started doing it too, oftentimes beating to the punch. *Che fai?!* I accuse Giro, who had whistled up to me from the window in my door. I don't feel guilty asking for a ride to town tomorrow to get the gas burner at the post office, now that I'm a card-carrying *brava ragazza*. He reaches through the window and taps me under the chin to say goodbye. My last taxi driver patted me on the top of my head. There's a much hazier divide between people here, which they express physically. There is no such thing as existing as a separate set of rights; you are also subject to judgement based on the effect you have on the homeostasis of the collective, and yet you receive its warmth in return.

Sicily 8/4/24

È una brutta giornata. Boiling hot, barely a breeze, and I myself have fallen into a trough where everything that yesterday seemed to have momentum, today has come to a grinding halt and I am staring at myself, figuratively speaking, wanting to throw my hands up and not do whatever it is I have to do to get out of this. Oh, it's always something deep, and difficult, and frightening, and I don't feel like it today with this weather. I've already spent the morning explaining to my taxi driver that I'm neither available nor interested, letting him down easy though because he knows where I live. You can't give anyone your number here for any purpose—all the drivers want to be texted directly so they don't have to give the boss his cut—without it turning into this. I can laugh at it now, because the situation has been diffused, but it's sort of like the day I got chased by the dogs, it's a reminder that I'm on my own here. Certain people, certain dogs, they know when you're on your own.

The only bright spot is that the new gas burner is a dream. I just put in a canister, turned it on and cooked, like at a modern house, a normal house, so to speak. I didn't have to collect wood, nor did it turn my upstairs into a sauna and cover the floor in bark and ash. Oh, all of my talk about the simple life, some of it was just talk.

I'm trying to remain neutral to this ennui. There's a whole philosophy of neutrality developing in my mind, something objective emerging out of my subjectivity.

Neutral is a better descriptor than *natural*, for my purposes here, even though for two months I've been banging on about nature. There are too many associations with the word natural, it's too easy to fool yourself into thinking something is good by calling it natural. Take tap water, for example, made up of fluoride, pesticides, and all of the pharmaceuticals people excrete. Water is natural. But that doesn't mean it is always neutral in the body.

The virtue of my simple diet here, of legumes, rice, beef, pears and apples, is that it is relatively neutral. The body will always return to homeostasis, that is the foundational truth of these incredibly complex living machines we have, and what is homeostasis but neutrality? Therefore, give it neutral conditions and neutral input so that it is not always being dragged away from neutrality to the point of malfunction.

In communication, too, there must be neutrality, which I realized recently after putting my foot in my mouth, roundly so, making my way through the thicket, revisiting the themes that were our undoing. Like the body, love is also, always, seeking homeostasis. This is true of all relationships, not just romantic. Any person who is relating to another person desires neutrality, because to ourselves we are neutral, and we want to be received as ourselves.

Fear, we allow fear to seep into all of our decision making and then everything gets misshapen and homeostasis gets harder and harder to maintain, or thrown out the window entirely. A person starts to feel sick, or love turns into constant bickering. An adventure that was designed to be difficult in a certain way turns into a tangle of problems and cannot bear its fruit.

Sicily 8/6/24

It's a jungle here, my whole body is sticky, anything that touches—hand and arm, leg and tablecloth—makes a *shhhlpp* sound when they come apart, and sweat drips down my back even when I'm not moving. We're in for several days of haze and humidity, though there have been a few cracks of thunder and I'm hoping it finally rains. The high water content of the air lends a silvery, shimmering quality to the drone of the cicadas.

My big excursion to town and the beach was three days ago, and it was glorious, seven hours laying in the sun and bathing in that resplendent water, but I will be back in the hills for a while. I have quite a lot to do, actually, now that the philosophy is in place to do some of what I said I was going to do. My walking days are over, my taxi days are over, but it's only three weeks until I will, in all likelihood, leave for Palermo. If I need to go to town sometime before I leave, I can get a ride both ways with my neighbor.

In the heat, I find myself laying with my guitar, like a sleeping *ragazzo*, plucking away, humming a tune, writing songs. If I write one every day, I'll have a collection of one-minute songs to bring into the studio, which is nice, which I can name *Sicily*. I brought the guitar along in the hopes that I would do something, anything, except that I didn't imagine the magic element would be my defenselessness against the humidity. And I shouldn't even be telling you this, because I have a habit of not finishing what I start. I suppose this is an attempt at accountability.

On this night last year I was the last one to arrive at my birthday dinner on the Upper East Side. My brother was sitting across from his latest girlfriend, and a then-acquaintance recently returned from a sojourn in Central Asia was sitting across from my empty seat.

Themes have a habit of annual return, I've learned over the years of recording my life. It could be any day of the year, it could be any idea, or person, or problem, but whatever comes into being will be back like clockwork 365 days later, or 730 days later, or 1,095 days later, or a hundred years later, in some form.

All of the latent pathos casting such a long shadow that night only revealed itself as a sudden pressure to iron out my life's problems as fast as humanly possible before they caused me to fumble and lose hold of this precious new creature. I failed miserably, of course, and it all exploded like bird shot. I walked blindly into having something to lose, straight out of my no-man's land where an old world and an old way of being had died, stumbling like a foot soldier who doesn't know what rules apply or what language to speak in this new country that he helped bring into existence.

But now I am somewhere peaceful where I can remember what peace is like, where everything is neutral. And I shouldn't excoriate myself for having ended up here on the anniversary of that first glimpse across the table, shyly fumbling with my purse, knowing in that moment I had nowhere left to hide.

Living, but only knowing what I was not, having no idea how to communicate what I am, never expecting that I could be received with understanding, or knowing how to receive another, such a way of living can't bear the weight of love. I knew it a year ago, but not what to do about it. If this was the only way that I could look at the matter squarely and figure out what to do, by following my vision to this island, then I have risen to the moment after all and did not shirk from my duty to him, or to life.

As I've already written, turning 34 begins a new phase of belonging to the world, not to where you have come from. Surprisingly, this new reality is actually present, in a lullaby, a phone call, and a shaky faith based on the scantest evidence that good will come.

Now it's time to go to lunch at Giro's house. Paranoid about whether I am fit to be inside a house with other people when my circumstances are so rudimentary, I scrub myself head to foot in the shower, check my clothes repeatedly for mustiness, and dab on perfume.

A birthday translation of Tsvetaeva from my sweet friend, who is in Normandy waiting for her fiance to come home from his night shift at the bottle factory:

August - asters	*Август — звёзды,*
August - stars	*Август — грозди*
August - clusters	*Винограда и рябины*
Grapes and rowan	*Ржавой — август!*
Rusty - august!	*Полновесным, благосклонным*
Full and kind	*Яблоком своим имперским,*
Held like apple	*Как дитя, играешь, август.*
By a child	*Как ладонью, гладишь сердце*
Emperor's name right from the start	*Именем своим имперским:*
As a hand print on the heart	*Август! — Сердце!*
August!	*Месяц поздних поцелуев,*
Tardy roses, kisses too	*Поздних роз и молний поздних!*
Lighting bolts with showers of stars	*Ливней звёздных —*
August!	*Август! —*
It rains fallen stars	*Месяц Ливней звёздных!*

Sicily 8/7/24

The rest of a pot of lentils went bad overnight since I ate lunch away from home yesterday. I brought them down to throw them out in the woods, and when I opened the door there were four brand new water jugs sitting there. I stepped over them and only on my way back did it occur to me who would have left them: the taxi driver. He had helped me get water from the spring and I told him that two of my jugs had leaks.

I opened my phone and pulled up the chat I had hidden in archive. Sure enough, a message telling me he had left the jugs, as well as an earlier invitation to go to a festival. *Thank you, you didn't have to do that, I don't want to spend time with you, take care,* I wrote, shaken up that he had been outside my house sometime last night without my even knowing it, perhaps while I was sleeping. I don't know whether he is really unhinged or just desperately lonely, and there's a fine line between pity and danger. I'm annoyed that right when everything starts to fall into place for me and I can envision returning home bearing a true gift to life, and continuing to write this travel diary, I'm questioning whether I should stay at all. But I don't want to forfeit just because some wretched person is trying to weasel their way into a place they're not wanted and not supposed to be.

Human relationship, and all the fine lines that we toe. If our needs are not met for too long, we go scorched-earth and destroy the possibility of having them fulfilled, turning into our own worst nightmare, accompanied by a set of delusions to protect ourselves from it. Yes, the caveat of the road to hell being paved with good intentions is that our intentions can all ultimately be traced back to ourselves and what we aren't getting. After all, if we were not in need, we would not act.

I was so in need of perspective, because everything was either not changing or getting worse, that I had to come all this way, for all this time.

But I joined Giro's family for lunch yesterday, since it was also his daughter's birthday, who is visiting from Milan with her Milanese fiance, who seems enormous among the petite Sicilians (even I am something of an amazon at five-and-a-half feet). I stayed for several hours, eating pasta and mussels, prickly pear and figs, and cake. Betta took me out onto the top floor balcony and pointed out the house where she grew up, and the house where Giro grew up, as the house he built for them—it turns out he was a builder, not a bricklayer—is right in the middle.

The humidity is down today, the heat has broken, the sun is shining, there is a pleasant breeze. I wonder if my tone will change throughout the month, now that the person to whom all of this is really addressed knows my pseudonym, and I know he is reading. I sang him a song on the phone the other night and he said, *That sounds like it's about me*, and I said, *It's also about God, it's about both of you*, which gets to the heart of the problem that I have always had with most of the present-day folk genre—there is so much potential to express the depth and breadth of human subjectivity, but it is all so firmly embedded in the here-and-now as if life were only a series of events and impressions. I don't believe that about life.

That doesn't mean I know whether I'll write anything of value, but I'm glad that I can combine these two yearnings, for the one who is far away, and for the Eternal One, because I don't see how they could ever be separated. The music and poetry I love most all came about at a time when no one even thought to separate them, but the level of importance given to each of them was balanced, and they remained respectfully intertwined. (Then the Great War snapped the golden thread between heaven and earth.)

The afternoon is getting on. I have to work on the translation, and shave my legs, and heat water to wash my socks and tank tops, and I have to do the dishes. Yesterday when I got back from lunch at Giro's big, spotlessly clean house, walking into my house was like going back in time. I didn't realize how much of my own little world I was in here, in the *rifugio*, I've just grown so used to it, to the stone walls, the primitiveness, and entire days where I speak to no one.

Sicily 8/8/24

I am Mary of the Seven Sorrows today, with the seven swords piercing her heart. Waiting for the sun to go down.

We cannot choose which day will be the longest, and which night the darkest: suddenly, they have come.

We follow a path, thinking it will be possible to turn back at any time, but a broom has swept our footprints away behind us.

Onward, as summer wanes. The chestnuts are turning yellow and dropping their fruit, the hazelnuts too. I meet people in the forest collecting the burrs to take home to shell.

I pace the forest at dawn, and again in late morning, up and down, up and down, up and down, and again in the afternoon. My legs ache in the evening sitting in the window.

I try to eat, but the food sits in the pots all day, only a spoonful here and there, and will go to waste.

Now I know everything there is to know. Has the time come to go home? But is that a place and can I go there?

There is no home, there is only Sicily, and the evening bells ringing out across the sea. God will provide, I tell myself.

Love is not evaporating and dissipating, it is blowing in on the evening wind. How? Because I asked it to, because I am never hopeless, because it is real like the wind, it can't be mistaken for anything else.

Sicily 8/10/24

Greetings from the windowsill on a glorious afternoon. The sun doesn't arrive on this side of the house until mid-afternoon, so I am sitting in the shade and a perfect, near constant breeze is playing in the elderberry tree. The village is still. The family across the street left at 6:00 this morning to go somewhere, which woke me, but at the moment I have this end of the street to myself. Usually, their voices form the caricature of a Sicilian family, impossible to differentiate between their emotions because everything they say is loud and impassioned, and half-drowned out by the clanking of dishes as they cook and eat.

Yesterday I got my act together and cleaned up the house. There was a bucket with a month's worth of wood ash that I had to get rid of, so I took the rinse water from my laundry and poured it in, just in case there was a stray ember. I then stuck my hands in and mixed it around for a few minutes to ensure everything was wet. It turns out that mixing wood ash and water forms lye, so I am looking down at my hands as I write, and they're starting to peel. I guess I learned my lesson.

This morning, I went to town on a whim with Giro, who had to buy feed for his chickens. We stopped for a macchiato and at the tabaccheria for lottery tickets, then he dropped me at the beach. I put down my things among the throng of families and dove straight into the ocean. A half hour later I had to get dressed, and we drove back up the mountain, stopping at the butcher in the lower village on the way so I could get lamb chops. It was the perfect expression of the month of August here, after all of the grandiosity of the long journey has mellowed and I am practically at the point of counting down the hours until I will have to take my leave.

Everyone is talking about collecting hazelnuts and chestnuts, which is what I think I will do during my walk this afternoon. The forest path is almost dangerous to walk down due to all of the nuts on the ground, and Alina had warned me about this, that in the autumn it's easy to slip and fall on them. The men have been busy cutting the grass in all of the groves, around the nut trees, around the olive trees, forming a carpet of sweet-smelling hay as it dries in the sun. But today is Saturday, so the air is quiet while people rest and go to the ocean.

I feel saturated with calm this afternoon, and look forward to these peaceful last weeks on this peaceful hillside. On a day like today, it is brought to bear upon me why we must always follow our intuitions, and act against them at our own peril: there is no other way to find what you seek, no other way to stop ducking and weaving, no other way to understand what it is you need to understand but are afraid of understanding.

Sicily 8/11/24

Last night I went for another walk down the forest path as dusk fell, the sky over the ocean hazy and mottled pink. My hair was laying on my neck, a sweat breaking out despite the relatively cool air, and as I left the village and entered into the woods, the same silvery tone of cicadas began to swell and ebb in the valley. I took a bunch of green grapes from the side of the road and ate them as I walked, my method being that I separate the small clusters from the main cluster, put the whole of it in my mouth, and strip it with my teeth. The grapes are small, and at this point nearly overripe. On the way back, no one was around so I took an enormous fig from the enormous tree across from the enormous house at the village end, which is alive with insects that I think are boring into the fruit. There must be a thousand figs on this tree.

È stata una bella estate, I keep saying to myself. It was a nice summer.

I took the same walk tonight, although shorter because it was so close to nightfall. A crescent moon hung over the Nebrodi, the heavens the color of blush roses, fading into the darkened hills topped with old, glowing cities. The last bunch of grapes, and a fig for dessert.

Everyone stopped by my door tonight, Giro and his daughter and son in law Lorenzo and their baby with the brown saucer eyes. I hung out the door window for a while, then my neighbor across the way appeared with a watering can to water his herbs out front, and the men stood there talking about the empty house, my walled garden. I joined them in the street, talking a while about who owns what, following along as best I could. I invited them in to see my house, not knowing who has been inside, since we were standing there talking about the properties, so they came in and looked around, and talked some shit, a favorite Sicilian pastime—*the guy who owns the house didn't keep it tidy like this, and his partner, she'd just change her clothes in her van, out in the street, and before you got here there were two men on motorcycles and they were gay!*

Outside again, Lorenzo handed me his leather pouch of tobacco and I rolled a cigarette to smoke with the men, then we walked down to the corner to fill up the water jugs the taxi driver bought me. All summer I've been told I can get water from somewhere close to my house, but every time I asked, Giro never knew what I was talking about. It turns out there's a spigot with a hose right there at the end of the street. Betta came out on the balcony, her sister came walking up the road to join the festivities, and she speaks a smattering of English, so any time a word came up that she knew, she would turn to me and translate. For a while, we all sat there as they talked and I listened, one person on a cinder block, another on a tree stump, me on a low wall.

Thank God, because I really needed a shower, but I was out of wash water and wasn't expecting visitors. I hadn't bathed since I'd been in the ocean yesterday, all the while sweating and sweating and sweating, wearing the same shirt for the third day in a row. Maybe that's why they insisted on getting me water.

A nice end to a long day of editing, moving from chair, to bed, to window, to chair, to floor, and cracking hazelnuts between two pieces of beach granite.

During my strolls through the forest, while hazelnuts fall onto the road around me with a clack, I've been ruminating on what makes love the force that it is. Not that *love conquers all*, rather, love as the great destroyer. Love binds us at first imperceptibly and then irrevocably, time and again testing our limits of endurance, understanding, patience, our sanity and our defenses. Love is the great Hell-harrower, the bottom-dredger. The only question it will ever ask of you is how much you're willing to sacrifice to not lose it, whether that be love of a person, or a place, something that you do or believe. And how often a confusion sets in at the moment of sacrifice, while you tally the costs to yourself. Nevertheless, you'll pay up in one way or another, either a flat rate now or down the line with interest.

But why else are we on earth? And what a reward love is when we emerge from the trials it puts us through.

Sicily 8/13/24

I don't know if I've been roped into a bit of theater, standing there waiting for my espresso. This is a nice establishment, with a wooden bar and a full case of pastries, painted Sicilian pottery adorning the shelves, and the barkeep in a crisp shirt. It's at the edge of town where the rural routes from the hillsides meet and it's always busy. As usual, I'm the only woman. Everyone else is male, deeply tanned, and in no hurry to get anywhere.

Ah yes, the woman in the red tube top and peasant skirt, the gold necklace and braided hair, sunglasses on her head, barely able to speak Italian, she fits right in. *You're related?* the barkeep says to Giro, smirking. He pauses, and then answers truthfully, *No, she's my neighbor,* which sounds so ridiculous that the barkeep shoots me another look and I can see that he feels his suspicions have been confirmed. Far from being ashamed, I really just want to laugh, but instead I open a packet of sugar and pour it into my little coffee cup and stir it around to busy myself. The men put on a disinterested machismo with each other, so there's no chance that Giro is going to save my honor and start making small talk about how I'm from America and living in his village, no way, so the assumptions just hang in the air.

When in Rome.

We continue into town and then part ways. I have just enough time to buy groceries and take a swim in the ocean. As usual, the water is resplendent, a kind of heaven on earth. We take a different route home that meanders through one of the charming hilltop cities that I've so often admired from far away, because he has to bring flowers to the cemetery where his parents are interred. By noon, I'm back at the *rifugio* dipping biscuits into leftover coffee.

Naturally, I consider the autonomy I've enjoyed my whole adult life and I wouldn't trade it. But back home, never once was I mistaken for an escort just by walking into a coffee shop. And there, I think something's been lost.

I understand now why nearly everyone has asked me if I'm married immediately after meeting me. It's part of my overall thesis about Sicily and its preservation of natural law. The mysterious, generative magnetism of the female animal is one of those laws. Here, it is still understood that woman has the capacity to enchant, that there is a strange magic to her, and that is why man must claim and defend. How strange, indeed, that I am free to roam about like an unbottled genie, that I would make it so many years without anyone trying to contain me.

It will be interesting to return home, knowing what I know now about life on earth.

Sicily 8/17/24

An empty quiet has fallen over the island. The forest floor is a bed of ripe nuts and brown leaves. Thunder rolls in the distance from time to time, and it would be a huge relief if it actually rained instead of drizzling. I imagine this is a foretaste of Sicily in the winter, when the exuberance of summer is gone and everything lies half-dormant, but not dead.

All of my worries have faded, and what is left is solitude and tranquility for a little longer. I don't know where the time has gone, and I don't know how I did it, how I actually got myself out of the rut I came here to get myself out of. What did I do but live here quietly? But then, when I go back and read what I was writing even before I left in May, how prescient it all was. Maybe the answers are always right in front of our faces like that, but they're usually easier to ignore or brush away. Maybe this will teach me that if I can accept being engulfed by the unknown for some time, not knowing what to do doesn't really exist. What exists is only the avoidance of letting the answers you already know unfold.

Maybe life is less a series of ups and downs, and more a series of lights preceded by darkness. Day becomes night which becomes day again, but we resist when night falls on the mind or heart, as if we didn't trust that the sun would rise again and that sleep had its purpose. That's all that it is, and it only takes the wrong weather to bring on a day of night—but the darker it is, the more welcome dawn will be, because there is a balance to them and they are in equal measure.

The trepidation attached to returning home is that this peace might slip through my fingers. I don't know why I have this fear, considering that the peace itself isn't tied to the fact that I am here. Sicily brought about the changes that I wanted to see before I left, and I can take those with me, even if this is only the threshold. It's nagging at me that some thought wants to break through before I leave, and it would, if only I let it.

I heard it said somewhere that little children and the elderly get along, even resemble each other, because they're closest to the other side. So it is at the end of journey, and my thought patterns are starting to resemble my arrival, and this place that I embraced so wholly at the peak of the summer is losing its familiarity. I've started to pack up the things I'm not using, in the suitcase my *ragazzo* lent me at the laundromat so long ago, and yet not that long ago. Little by little removing the traces of my ever having been here. My thoughts often wander to the yards of Indian cotton that should have arrived in Pennsylvania by now, and I've made the shirts over and over again in my mind.

The night itself is dark, the stars obscured, no breeze to rustle the leaves, not even the buzzing of insects, while a dog barks in the distance. Before nightfall I went down to the spring and arrived at the same time as someone else. He let me go first, then proceeded to collect handfuls of hazelnuts and break them open with a rock while he waited. We didn't say anything to each other, I just filled my bottles and said good night, and ate red grapes from the roadside on the way home.

Sicily 8/18/24

By its very nature, the experience of time is an experience of uncertainty. It's not a good thing to become unaccustomed to this, because that's how a person turns into a useful idiot for whatever forces prey upon insecurity. It's strange, but true, that it's much easier to destroy what you love (your life, your relationships, your country) than it is to patiently accept that the contemplation of your own existence is enough to keep you busy for twenty lifetimes. As this century wears on, man seems to be less and less capable of relinquishing his infantile omnipotence. But why should he? Water and warmth appear at the turn of a dial, he witnesses plenty every week at the supermarket, he can even absorb opinions without having to form his own.

Yet civilization itself is a response to uncertainty, increasingly intricate solutions to common problems. Take away uncertainty, and you take away the meaning of life.

Modernity was supposed to free us to attend to ever higher pursuits, but in reality we've gone from building monuments to the contemplation of what we cannot see, to contemplating what we can see and denying it. How did we fall so low, so quickly?

I bring it up because I think that's the nagging thought, and I think this is my last Sicilian hurdle. Getting home requires so many impossible things to happen, like getting from this hillside to a city 100 miles away where there's a big tin can that's going to fly me across thousands of miles of open ocean, that I keep ignoring what's in front of me. I keep trying to distract myself from experiencing time, frittering it away until it's time to sleep. But the important point to make is that this isn't out of fear, it's that in this situation I can't pretend that everything is under my control. By my own logic, I'm taking the meaning out of my own final days here by being unable to sustain my solitude in the face of a future point of unpredictability, when in fact, that very uncertainty is the kernal of my capacity to edify the raw material of my time.

And that's only one example of an uncertainty. This little thought is probably the key to the next decade or more.

This afternoon I had to try to put an old wine barrel back together. It was being used as a table upstairs, but collapsed inward when I pushed the lid down on a container of olives, way back in June when I first arrived. Now I'm just covered in dust from sitting on the floor in the basement, the day is almost over, and it was impossible. I put fifty euros in an envelope and tucked it into the bucket full of barrel pieces. I assume it came with the house and I feel terrible, but at least I've relieved myself of the duty to attempt fixing it.

Sicily 8/19/24

Last night a massive thunderstorm erupted. The *rifugio* even shook a couple of times, while water dripped from a leak in the roof. On and on it went, this storm, the sky flashing purple with each burst of lightning. In this old, old house, alone, thinking of Mount Etna spewing lava on the southern coast of the island, the storm felt like a communication of heavenly unrest and displeasure. Did the animals feel it coming? The night before while I lay in bed falling asleep, all the dogs in the valley were barking, even howling, and I thought to myself—that can't be good. What do they know that we don't?

It rained and rained and rained, it just kept raining. For once, I appreciated the horribly placed skylight above my bed, which is right under a street lamp. It was like an animation of raindrops that I was watching from underneath the surface of a pond. It was raining at sunrise, but when I finally got out of bed later in the morning, the sky was spectacularly clear and I could even see the houses and shifts in vegetation on the islands off in the distance. It was like waking up to a new world.

It turns out it is possible to fix an old wine barrel. I couldn't really leave it broken, it belongs to the house. I tried many methods, but the one that worked was to lay out the pieces and line them up in the order they seemed to fit in. Then I tied a rope along the length, to each individual piece, top and bottom, to connect them. From there, I could roll them up into a barrel shape, and with a wreath of hazelnut wood to maintain the tension on the inside, get the pieces aligned so that I could drop the largest hoop down. Then I fitted the bottom of the barrel in, and slid the other two hoops down, hammering the top one into place to tighten it. Tomorrow I'll get a few more hazelnut shoots to bend into hoops to reinforce it from inside. I can't tell you how pleased I am with myself.

Unfortunately, a nearby village is having a festival which means terrible dance music is blaring, so despite being exhausted from coopering all day, there's no chance that I'll be able to sleep until it's over.

Sicily 8/20/24

As the days here tick by leading up to my departure, as more thunderstorms roll through and I watch the clouds gather over the churning, bright turquoise ocean, the more far away I feel. Fixing the wine barrel has brought a sense of completion to my life in the *rifugio*, which is what made me keep trying, because I knew it was a symbolic act. (We don't break anything that we aren't also meant to learn how to fix.) But my little jaunt with planes, trains and automobiles is seeming facile to me, if you think that people used to sail off into the distance on wooden ships looking for the ends of the earth.

Reading the tabloids last night to pass the time until the dance music ended, I saw a headline about a tornado on the water sinking a yacht just west of here near Palermo during the storm the other night; of the six missing are a lawyer from New York and his wife. It was a huge storm that also flooded our little town at the bottom of the hills, but I was safe and warm in my house watching the raindrops from my bed, with no idea of the destruction going on elsewhere. Once again, I've been saved by my relative poverty.

There was also an article about the Shroud of Turin being dated with some sort of x-ray to the time of Christ, which got me thinking that maybe Turin is the next place I will spend a season, someday. After a Christmas in Genoa several years ago, I've often dreamt of returning to northern Italy in the winter and walking through the cool, dry air, closer to where the other half of my mother's family comes from. The train from Bern passed through the snow covered mountains and emerged in a different land, with a layover in Domodossola, where all of the old women had the same knobby knees as my grandmother, before continuing on to Genoa. I stayed in a room in a grand old apartment building with terrazzo floors, and the city was almost empty that time of year. All of the orange trees were heavy with fruit.

And if I know anything at this point in my life, it's that every worthwhile journey always begins with an image, a seemingly random need.

Waking out of a deep sleep to the blustery weather this morning, the Shroud swimming in my consciousness, felt so pure that it evoked the unmediated contentment of childhood, taking in life through the sensations without any irony. It also makes it a good day to finish the song I started during the storm, the fourth one.

I risked a walk to the spring earlier, primarily because I wanted grapes, and got caught in the rain on the way back. Summer wanes more every day, the trees are tinged with yellow and the bed of leaves in the hazelnut groves grows thicker, as autumn sets in, in earnest. I might have to build a little fire tonight to warm up the room to sleep. When the sky cleared in the afternoon, I set out into the forest and still had to wait out a shower under the canopy of a chestnut, but made it back to my ancient door and the warm pot of lentil soup, past the sweet smell of rotting figs that had been knocked to the ground by the rain at the end of the village.

On my walk, the concept of uncertainty started to meld with the image of God's face, making me think that if uncertainty is the factor that eventually develops into what we know as culture which eventually becomes high culture, it has to be balanced out by a certainty of the same depth, otherwise everyone who ever existed would simply descend into a state of psychosis, finding existence unbearable. The only match for the fact that we cannot see into the future is something else that we cannot see. To live with the knowledge that we will die and do not know when, that we don't even know what tomorrow will bring, there has to exist something that cannot die, and knows neither tomorrow nor yesterday nor present: The Eternal One.

There is something that I cannot see that is eternal. If we do not feel this at our very core, we will spend our lives managing an unrelenting, nagging uncertainty that we aren't even aware of. Because if we were aware of it, we would have to recognize God, and not everyone wants to do that, especially not anymore.

Our ability to transcend, truly, exists in between the two poles. Wherever or however that takes place in a person's life isn't my business, but I feel certain of this. The gilded interior of the Aachen Cathedral for instance, a truly unforgettable sight, does not exist at the polarity of glorification, no, because if men were that certain there would be no need to build it, and if they existed at the other polarity, perhaps as nihilistic biological determinists, they wouldn't have bothered. The pressure of the two poles exerting their forces upon man pushes him into the center and then upward.

But a cathedral is an example of a collectivist undertaking, with many lives coming and going in the process and artisans working together to form a masterwork, which doesn't happen anymore. So I can really only speak for the smaller instances of transcendence that happen in individual lives, such as my own little life.

I don't recall where I read the passage, but the writer was observing people on a train, and watched how shortly after leaving the station, they started pulling out their sandwiches and eating, with the whole journey still ahead, to comfort themselves. Something like that, reaching for gratification straight away and not being able to put it off for when you're really hungry, because the unknown can be so disturbing.

Sicily 8/22/24

An almost unbearable restlessness has taken hold of me, but I don't know where it's coming from, nor what it's directing me towards. Sleep has been difficult, I toss and turn, during the day I can't think straight, can't concentrate on anything. But I've started preparing to leave; cleaned the bathroom, raked the loose stones on the first floor back to where they belong with my hands and smoothed it out with my feet, washed the jeans and sweater that I'll wear on the plane and laid them on the roof of an abandoned house to dry in the sun, hemmed some towels that I'll leave behind.

But then I go to the sea, and at the sea I forget all my troubles. No one here calls it the beach, or the ocean. It's the sea, *il mare*. Two days ago, after running my morning errands, like stopping in at the Church of The Annunciation on the main street, buying fruit and illegally getting rid of my trash, I waited out a shower under an awning with a toddler in her grandfather's arms, chattering away about the rain. *But the rain is nice, my head is getting wet!* he said to her. The sky cleared and I made it to the near-empty beach where I had to wait out another shower, this time under a palm tree while I ate grapes. Then the sky cleared again, the beach filled with people, white cumulus clouds amassed above us, and I swam for *un'oretta*, a little hour, in the choppy waves. It's still summer down at sea level, with maybe just a slight bite to the wind.

Sicily 8/23/24

Awake to watch the sun rise this morning, walked to the spring before 7:00, not many people about now that the mornings are a little cooler for a little longer. Sleep temporarily washed away the disquietude of the past few days, but by mid-morning I'm on edge again, jumping when I hear a gecko in the dry leaves, wanting to scream if the teenager across the street makes his mother call his name one more time without coming downstairs. In truth, it's the end of the month, but I'm not usually so alone with myself. Usually there's someone to snap at, or a fight to pick, or I can yell at the dog for barking, or drive to the store and get road rage.

But the veil begins to lift somewhat as the thoughts arrange themselves into an intelligible whole. What I want is to talk to someone, not in the literal sense, but in the sense of communion, *coniunctio*, a melding, a release from my solitude, forever.

When I went to put my sweater and jeans back out on the roof of the abandoned house today, I wondered how it would be said in Italian, that nothing wants to dry in this humidity. Nothing *wants* to dry. What a ridiculous construction, as if the damp sweater had a say in the matter. But then, we use *Do you want to…* as a soft command, where the subject also has no agency. Then there is *to be in want*, which is to be lacking, where it is again implied that the subject can't do anything about it, or even whining *I want to sleep* when you can't sleep. And yet if you were to ask me to define the verb *to want*, I would describe it in a more positive sense, of intending to attain something.

I want communion, but what I'm really saying is that I don't have it because I've rejected it. I reject the books I brought, and in fact I have always rejected reading because it pains me somehow, and I rejected properly learning Italian this summer, so I have no one to read, no one to talk to. What is this? It's easy to follow through on wanting when it is an intuition that requires one big decision, like just showing up here, when the rest is up to fate. It's much harder when that intuition is a nagging one that you need to be chipping away at slowly, that requires you to make the same decision a thousand times. It's like an insomnia of being.

I want to, but I can't. I want to, but I don't know how. *Voglio ma non posso. Voglio ma non so come.* What I do instead is peel and eat six pears in one sitting. But this is it, this is what I am, this is that mundane something that is what I am —

— this is the return, this is the circle closing.

It's so much easier to hold someone else in contempt, to be the eagle to their Prometheus, to peck away at their liver for an eternity when all they wanted was to bring a spark of fire to earth. I know I wrote about that when I first arrived, maybe even before I left, bringing something to earth out of the sky. The image comes back to me now in this much darker form, because I've realized it takes a lot more courage than I want it to, a lot more clarity of purpose, I have to actually face off with the divine and risk something. I can sit in my window and stare at the sky all I want, can't I?

Sicily 8/25/24

So thick was the haze of humidity that there was no moon last night, there were no stars, no islands, and the town on the far hill appeared to be floating in space. A car coming down the road was just an orb of light moving slowly, slowly across the black.

Many years ago when I was a student, and had buzzed off all my hair when that sort of thing was still rebellious, I went on a weekend trip to the Dalmatian coast with friends. We were studying in Germany at the time (which mostly meant picnicking and going dancing). Night was falling as we took a ferry back to the mainland from an island where we had gone swimming for the day, and the hills were flickering with light as the scattered villages responded to the coming darkness. Every once in a while over the ensuing years, I would see a hillside at dusk glimmering with human habitation, but only rarely, and would think of that moment on the ferry and how it had moved me so deeply. In the village here, I've been very lucky to watch this happen every evening, and it still moves me, and I wonder why, and I wonder if that is what brought me here.

Spirits are higher today. Yesterday morning I caught a ride to town with Giro. The market where I buy fruit now has three people manning its tiny produce section, but they do have the best fruit and it's always busy. The pears are exquisite, not quite like the figs, but a close second. I managed a short swim in the ocean, which is a little colder every time now. Espresso, fruit, ocean, and then back home, which I'll get to do maybe once more before I leave. The barista, with her blue eyeliner, told me with a wink I could work for her if I come back to Sicily. These people, they're always surprised when I say I'm leaving, as if it were understood that, once here, I would stay. Two different men have very sincerely offered to have me come live with them, because I'm alone and they're offering, so why wouldn't I? What's so complicated about it?

Departure is approaching rapidly. I think that this will be my first homecoming where there is no crisis brewing, where in fact, it almost feels triumphant. The past *as it was* is dead and buried, and it is I who twisted its neck. I'll be back in the same rooms, with the same people, doing the same things, but I'm not the same, in some way. I can't put myself in the shoes that I was wearing three, four, five months ago. I know what I was thinking and feeling then, but they might as well be someone else's memories.

Let me try to put that succinctly, what I mean. I return bearing the eternal flame of my existence, and I understand that I have to protect it from the wind. It was always burning, but the winds were often strong and the oil was low, and yet I saw the problem in the flame itself, not in the wind, not in the oil, not in the wick. Why that was doesn't matter anymore. What matters is that the instinct of preservation has kicked back in. I've never lived that way before, freely, thinking that maybe my life is a good thing, that I can do something with it other than fighting it, day in day out.

But I also came to a disconcerting realization. I came here to be in solitude so I could get a grip on myself, to not have anybody around reflecting me back to myself in any way, or needing me to reflect them back to themselves. And then I come here and I expect the hills to reflect back to me that I am someone who can be moved by them, and if I am not moved, I am bitter towards the hills. But the hills exist regardless of whether I am looking at them and they owe me nothing. The same is true of people, we treat each other like looking glasses, constantly interrupting the other person's right to be what they are.

It's frightening when you start looking around—the tree, the socks drying on the laundry line, the basket of fruit, the broom in the corner—and thinking about how it's all there, and none of it cares if I'm here, and the indifference of the objects towards my existence makes them seem alive. Their indifference endows them with being. I think this is one of the higher expressions of love, to allow something to be indifferent towards you, to allow it to exist and needing nothing in return.

What a lovely parting gift from Sicily, to bring all the world to life.

Sicily 8/26/24

Afternoon crept up on me yesterday, but I had a last minute translation job that took me until the wee hours to finish, when the roosters started crowing. I slept a little, and then woke early anyway. The *rifugio* was filled with the pleasant scent of Marseilles soap from all of the laundry I had boiled over the gas stove; underwear, socks and towels, shirts that had gotten musty when they refused to dry earlier this week. Boiling does the trick, just as good as a washing machine. I was trying to take a nap when Giro whistled, and I called down that I was sleeping, so he let himself in and came up the ladder, offered me a cigar, made small talk for a few minutes, asked me what time I want to leave for the train station on Thursday, and then I sent him on his way to the forest where he was going to get hazelnuts. Afterward, though, I did fall asleep until dinnertime.

This morning was my last trip to the beach for the summer. Not a cloud in the big, blue sky, and my heart was filled with sorrow, saying goodbye to this stretch of the Sicilian coast. A flock of little girls were with their mothers in the water next to me, their shining faces beaming, in total harmony with existence, at one with their own Madonnas. One of them stood up on a boogie board that her mother was holding steady in the water while the other girls chanted *Giulia! Giulia!* The Latin roots of the language are most charming in the mouths of babes, they haven't yet taken on the harshly expressive Sicilian cadence, and so they speak like little marble cherubim from an ancient world. *Quindi* this and *quindi* that.

I will miss this place. Not a care in the world right now, which is a bit of grace considering that I do actually have a lot of cares, only they're on the other side of the ocean. But as they say, *piano piano*, softly softly, little by little, and the life I will lead from this point forward is not the one I would have led if I had never come here.

Uncertainty, and grace. You can't have one without the other.

I wonder if, after a while in America, Sicily will come to mind and I'll think that it's about time I was getting home to the island. I don't think I'm done with this place, after all, I didn't see a single one of the big cities.

Sicily 8/28/24

Cleaning the house today.

Physical reality is quite static, and a lot of the good in life comes from the maintenance of a good to prevent it from slipping into decay. It's fairly easy to see what is beautiful and should be maintained. The strong iconoclastic bent of post-war America, which has engaged in such psychopathy as tearing down the original Penn Station, is an amoral, at times actively sinister, force. There *is* such a thing as an ideal balance between man and nature, and while it *is* harder to find under its modern wrapping, it *is* there, and it *is* the source of the good. It is the *bai hui*, the crown of the head where heaven and earth meet.

My neighbor called up to me through the door window, so I came down. It sounded like he was saying *Wäsche*, which makes no sense except that all summer I've been mixing German into Italian, when my mind starts grabbing at the first foreign language it knows. It turned out he was saying *pesce*. A man was driving around in a Fiat selling smelts from the back of his car and he had parked just outside my house. He'd even remove the heads for me if I wanted him to, I could tell, by the bucket of fish heads. My mouth was watering. But in the middle of cleaning the last thing I want to do is fry fish, so I had to decline.

A storm is rolling in. They always roll in from the south and move towards the ocean. More often than not, however, the thunder rumbles all afternoon and the humidity never breaks.

I take a particular pleasure in cleaning places that I'm leaving for good. Leaving no trace is its own trace left. I usually think about it for a week or two before I do it, taking apart the room in my mind and deciding where to start, where to end. I don't know if it was ever explicitly stated by my mother, but her belief is that if you're not on your hands and knees, you're not really cleaning your floors, so I cleaned the floor like I've been taught. *If you go back to him, you'll be on your knees for the rest of your life*, I was told earlier this summer by one of the many old men who got fresh with me when I told him I had a *ragazzo* back home. Well, he's never met my mother and seen her clean the floors. I was going to be on my knees for the rest of my life anyway.

This summer has helped me come to peace with where I've come from. I had been in the U.S. for five years straight, the longest I'd gone since I first started traveling, and they were five years of confrontation with what had brought me to where I was in life. What the Germans call an *Auseinandersetzung*, a setting of things apart from each other.

I think, upon my return, I'll be better able to differentiate between the America that contains what I love, and the America that is a country gone astray, where there are a few too many forces acting against the good, against man.

The sky has suddenly grown very, very dark and huge gusts of wind are thrashing the forest about. I finished all of my cleaning, showered, then ran downstairs to shut the wooden windows against the storm. The house seems empty without my things everywhere. There's no rain, just an incredible wind blowing, while the Mediterranean is filled with white-peaked waves and lighting is striking the water.

As night falls, the wind has blown some of the clouds off the water, which are lit pink from below by the waning sun. Lights glimmer in the Aeolian Islands, and the smell of wood smoke is being carried into my room from a neighboring house. Life, my friends, is a miracle. It's comforting to know that in death we return to the wind, and all the bitterness of life dissipates.

Sicily 8/29/24

My second-to-last sunrise in Sicily, the last one at the *rifugio*. When the sun rises again, I'll be boarding a plane to Rome after spending the night in the airport. I'm not looking forward to it.

Giro picked me up at quarter past seven this morning to go to the bakery. *Come stai?* I said to him when I got in the car. *Solita vita*, was his response, same old life. I guess it doesn't matter where you spend your days, if you have a view of the Mediterranean, your own lemon trees, your family around you, almost seventy years on the same hillside will elicit a similar response to almost seventy years in most places. *Mi manchi*, he says, and in truth, I'll miss him too, his particular spark of life, and remain grateful to him, for without him I never could have stayed here all summer. I wonder how long my ghost will live at this house, when he passes by, as others come and go, the ghost of *gioia mia*.

What I didn't know about the bakery is that you have to go up to the open window out front and yell *Giuseppe!* to get bread. There's no storefront, which is why I could never figure it out on my own. The baker reached his hand through the window to shake mine and handed me two loaves of bread, still warm, three euros total. It's all I'm going to eat today until I get to Palermo after sunset, because I don't want to cook, and I started by dipping it into my remaining olive oil with salt this morning for breakfast.

When you stay in one place for a long time, you start to think that things have to be a certain way, that you have to be a certain kind of person, and do certain things, but anything past the Commandments is all kind of made up. It's good to know that I'm returning home with a lot more money than I thought I would have by now, and all of these notions about what life is for and what I'm supposed to be doing with my time on earth, they all got washed away in the sea.

To stretch my legs a little before the journey ahead, I walked to the spring and tried to imagine myself in Giro's position, if this had always been my life and always would be. I wonder if the island would feel small, being surrounded by water, knowing you can only go a few hours at most in any direction. I wonder if he ever dreamt of what lies beyond Sicily. But he's been married since he was twenty, so where was he going to go, and why? Who is the lucky one, Giro or me? The one who belongs to a place with every cell of his body, or the one who could go anywhere because her belonging is almost undefined? Would I have had the same consciousness if I had been born here, and what would that have meant for my life then? Who would I be, what would I talk about, if Italian were my mother tongue? What if I had never undergone all of the suffering that life in the New World brought about? I don't think I would be who I know myself to be.

On the train to Palermo now. The afternoon felt interminable, waiting at the house for the time to leave. Unfortunately, I think I live a lot of my life that way, as if I were waiting to leave. Wasn't it only a week or two ago I was traveling in the other direction, not knowing what was ahead of me? I'm out of sorts, nervous, like I snapped awake out of a dream. Giro waited on the platform with me, a cigar in the corner of his mouth as usual, and now I'm going back to everyone, everything that I knew, but don't know anymore, and yet know too well. How good it has been to have gotten away. If only I could keep my mind in Sicily while the rest of me returns to America.

Sicily to America 8/31/24

It was an uneventful ride to the airport. I could have left a lot later, but my nerves got the best of me. There were a surprising number of people spending the night there like myself, and a surprising number of them were sleeping on the floor. I don't understand the point of giving up your dignity for a few hours of sleep.

I opened Paddy Fermor's letters: "Darling Nancy, There's a horrible *scirocco* blowing here—ashen sky, mewing cats, slamming windows, and hearts of lead. The villagers, reduced to nervous phantoms by Lenten fasting, with several days to go still—we're halfway between Greek Palm Sunday and Easter—get snapper and snappier...By the time the paschal lambs are on their spits, they will be beyond everything except gnashing and scowling." I thought of the overcast days on the Mediterranean that I endured, my own gnashing and scowling, the fighting cats, the screeching rats in the walled garden at night, the shrill voice of the woman across the street yelling, *Vieni! Subito!*

Getting onto the plane in Palermo at dawn was chaos, barking matches kept breaking out between all of the lap dogs being carried around, and then I had to sprint through half of Rome Fiumicino, weaving through hordes of people at top speed with a guitar, to get on the plane to New York. But I made it, and I sat on the plane quietly for eight hours thinking of the conversation that had ended when I entered the air.

In Pennsylvania, I didn't make it to sundown before falling asleep. I woke in the dark feeling its essence, a distillation of the forces that created it: the climate and flora, the angle of the sun, the people that came or were brought here, the industries that have come and gone, the ways of speaking. This is no sunny village in Sicily, this is a valley in a deciduous forest out of which a city has been cut, and my family belongs to this place as assuredly as the moon belongs to night.

I looked around my room and saw all of the things I had left behind. I remembered why I bought them, all meant to solve some problem— that dress because I wasn't feeling beautiful, and those bottles of herbs because my body hurt, and the expensive bed sheets with lace edging because I was working on a farm and spending my days covered in mud, acting like a rough person around other rough people. Where are those problems now?

What we call materialism isn't anything that we chose for ourselves. We are human beings, after all, and we are still driven to solve our problems—the ability to do so is what makes us human—and we don't have many means here other than to try and buy our way out of a corner. Where is the bright hillside with the view of the sea that will heal me? Nowhere. Where are the ancient houses at the edge of the wood to remind me that life is fleeting? Nowhere. Where is my piece of land that brings forth lemons and olives and provides for me? Nowhere.

Oh crushing weight of what *is*, and yet in reality it is only what *seems to be*. This place where I was born, and to which I belonged for thirty-three years, is as specific a place on earth, as specific a place in time, as there ever was. What is sad about it, is that it came to be after the link between man and earth was broken, and so there are almost no traces here of human beings engaging with their world, it was all done by machine, by larger interests than a voice from within that says, *Do this*. A man can put his mark on things after the fact, but there are no reminders of his father's father's father's father's father's father's father's hand.

My heart aches for Sicily, that other place that felt like home, that became home for a part of me that couldn't live in the dark forests of the New World. The part of me that was always fighting, fighting, but in Sicily, didn't have to fight anymore. A message comes in from that other universe, *Quanto mi manchi*, life itself speaking to me through Giro, as if to say, that part of you has to keep on living, now that it has been known.

America 9/1/24

September. It's nice having a hot shower and a washing machine, though less exciting than I thought it would be. There was something about the struggle against heat and decay that made life feel more heroic in the *rifugio*. Scrubbing up with soap at the sink and then taking a sharp breath while I rinsed off under the icy spring water was always such a tender experience, it was something I was doing for myself, rather than to myself. I couldn't tell you what my shower was like after getting home from the airport last night, I've already forgotten.

Where has the horizon gone? Where is the sea?

The first thing I did today was drive north to the only fabric store that has anything good, an old Sew and Vac in the mountains with printed cottons based on 19th century shirting, and walked away with 16 yards. My father refinished my sewing table and took the machine in to the shop while I was away. I think Sicily was the first place I fit in wearing my own clothing. Not only because the women there are very feminine and put great effort into their appearance, but because the environment supports it too. Pluck any one of them out of Sicily and land her in an American suburb and the neighbors would avoid her, but she's so at home on an arid coast where cacti grow, where the bougainvillea put forth their fuschia leaves and the sea is the color of God's eyes (one can imagine).

We become what surrounds us. But maybe I can do otherwise, maybe I can live in this world but reflect a different one, a world with bougainvilleas and their tiny, secret flowers within.

I feel a new love for humanity, because I have seen what we are meant to do, not only what we do. Unable to decide on what sort of sleeve to cut for the first blouse, I sit and change the strings on my guitar. Running my thumb across them, still out of tune, the resonance is deeper and I understand the necessity of it all now, the necessity of doing something human, the necessity of bringing beauty into the world. We must be the vanguards of beauty, otherwise it goes away.

Outside the window, the night is alive with insects. I can feel how big America is, how wide, how tall.

September 13. Preparing to return to New York again, where I spent my first week back. How long? I don't know. It could be a day, it could be ten years. I came back to Pennsylvania to sew for a few days. When I want to make something, I become gripped with the obsession, and this has happened to me since I was a young girl. After so many years, with a needle and thread in hand I can do whatever I want. But when I finished the shirt and the dress and snapped back into reality, it was time to get back to the city.

I packed a big bag of things I might need to keep in my car. This has been my life for the past year, sort of living here and sort of living there, not really able to do everything I need to do or see everyone I need to see in one place. But at least, after Sicily, the world in general is a brighter place to me, so I know that it was right that I went there. And the understanding that life really is that simple, when it comes down to it, I've brought with me.

Giro wrote to say that he has been abandoned, but I never have time to answer him. Life in America is busy, and I've just started making the rounds of people I want to visit. I have invitations to New England, emails sitting unread, dates to set, shows to see. I didn't think I had a busy life, but now that I'm back, and more alive than I was before I left, my memories of Sicily are like a dream of the slowest place on earth.

September 14. I am no longer really here, no longer really where I am: I used to feel tied to the Earth, but I am not anymore. I am somehow still in my window looking out at the islands, taken out of time, completely free in the only way that one can be free, which is alone inside four stone walls, behind a wooden door with an iron lock. Taken out of time, having given up on the world as I knew it, I let it go—and we all know the old adage, that only in letting go of something can you see if it comes back to you.

I don't mean to say that I'm not afraid, or that I know what is to come, because I have no idea, and I have never known. But I don't care anymore, as if I had experienced being all spirit and seeing the matters of this world from far away, like watching the boats on the ocean from the mountainside.

My fears about returning were unfounded. I have returned, and now the world says to me, *All that I have is yours.*

THE END.

Serpent Club Press
SCP